GLUTEN
INTOLERANCE

Published in 2006 by Murdoch Books Pty Limited
www.murdochbooks.com.au

Murdoch Books Australia
Pier 8/9
23 Hickson Road
Millers Point NSW 2000
Phone: +61 (0) 2 8220 2000
Fax: +61 (0) 2 8220 2558

Chief Executive: Juliet Rogers
Publishing Director: Kay Scarlett

Design manager: Vivien Valk
Project manager: Emma Hutchinson
Editor: Zoë Harpham
Food consultant: Michelle Earl
Design Concept: Susanne Geppert
Designer: Anthony Vandenburg
Photographer: Ian Hofstetter
Stylists: Jane Collins and Katy Holder
Food preparation: Joanne Kelly and Grace Campbell
Recipes by: Michelle Earl and members of the Murdoch Books Test Kitchen
Production: Adele Troeger

National Library of Australia Cataloguing-in-Publication Data

Holt, Susanna.
Eat well live well ... with gluten intolerance: gluten-free recipes and tips.

Includes index.
ISBN 978 1 74045 960 0.
ISBN 1 74045 960 1.

1. Gluten-free diet – Recipes. I. Title. (Series: Eat well live well; 1).
641.56318

Printed by Sing Cheong Printing Co. Ltd. in 2006. PRINTED IN HONG KONG.

The Publisher and stylist would like to thank Dinosaur Designs, Mud Australia, Bison Homewares and IKEA for assistance in the photography of this book.

IMPORTANT: Those who might be at risk from the effects of salmonella poisoning (the elderly, pregnant women, young children and those suffering from immune deficiency diseases) should consult their doctor with any concerns about eating raw eggs.

CONVERSION GUIDE: You may find cooking times vary depending on the oven you are using. For fan-forced ovens, as a general rule, set the oven temperature to 20°C (35°F) lower than indicated in the recipe. We have used 20 ml (4 teaspoon) tablespoon measures. If you are using a 15 ml (3 teaspoon) tablespoon, for most recipes the difference will not be noticeable. However, for recipes using baking powder, gelatine, bicarbonate of soda (baking soda), small amounts of flour and cornflour (cornstarch), add an extra teaspoon for each tablespoon specified.

EATWELLLIVEWELL

with GLUTEN
INTOLERANCE

Gluten-free recipes and tips

Introductory text by Dr Susanna Holt (PhD, Dietitian)

MURDOCH BOOKS

CONTENTS

LIVING WITH GLUTEN INTOLERANCE

A diagnosis of gluten intolerance no longer means the end of delicious foods. With the range of gluten-free products now available it is easy to follow a gluten-free diet, and with all the simple recipes in this book there are gluten-free meals for every occasion.

Who Will Benefit From This Book?

This book has been designed to provide people who need to follow a gluten-free diet, and those who cater for them, with important information about coeliac disease and dermatitis herpetiformis (DH), as well as provide practical advice on healthy gluten-free eating. If you suspect you have coeliac disease or DH it is important that you consult a qualified doctor for diagnosis. Once you have been diagnosed, it is recommended that you join your local coeliac or DH organization. These organizations can provide invaluable support and practical advice and refer you to an expert dietitian, which is particularly beneficial in the early stages after diagnosis.

How Can This Book Help?

This book contains a broad range of tested gluten-free recipes that are relatively quick and easy to prepare. There are recipes for everyday eating and special occasions. Meals with a low glycaemic index (GI), which produce a relatively small rise in blood-sugar level after they are eaten, have also been included for people who have both coeliac disease and diabetes. There are plenty of recipes that will suit the whole family; so if you only have one family member who requires a gluten-free diet, you won't need to prepare different meals. Preparing gluten-free meals that the whole family can enjoy is particularly valuable if you have a child who requires a gluten-free diet because it's important to make them feel as though they're being treated like the rest of the family (it also has the other benefit of saving you time).

Why Follow A Gluten-Free Diet?

Gluten is a type of protein found in wheat, barley, rye, triticale and oats. For some unknown reason, gluten causes an immune reaction in people with coeliac disease or DH that damages their small intestine and impairs normal digestive processes. While it can be initially challenging to switch to a gluten-free diet and to come to terms with your condition, it's important to remember that following a gluten-free diet is less difficult than the treatment needed for many other health conditions and there are lots of resources available to help you. The growing number of people with

coeliac disease has led the food industry to develop an increasing range of gluten-free convenience foods. It is becoming easier to find safe gluten-free foods in supermarkets and health-food stores, or you can order them from specialist food companies over the internet. Eating a gluten-free diet is much easier now than it was 20 years ago, but it can still be challenging at times, particularly when you are first becoming used to the diet.

What Is Coeliac Disease?

Coeliac (pronounced *seeliac*) disease is a condition where the body is not able to tolerate the protein gluten. When people with coeliac disease consume gluten, their immune system overreacts and the lining of their small intestine becomes damaged. The entire inner surface of the small intestine is lined with millions of tiny finger-like projections called villi, which absorb water and nutrients from digested food matter as it passes through the small intestine. In people with coeliac disease, the body's adverse immune reaction to gluten causes the villi to become inflamed and flattened. Without normal villi, the body is less able to absorb water and nutrients from digested food. As the villi become progressively more damaged in people with untreated coeliac disease, they can suffer from various stomach and bowel problems and nutrient deficiencies. Coeliac disease is both an autoimmune disorder (because the body's immune system causes the damage) and a digestive disease (because nutrient absorption is impaired).

Common symptoms of coeliac disease include:

- excessive gas (flatulence), abdominal pain and bloating
- chronic diarrhoea; pale, foul-smelling or fatty stools
- nausea, vomiting
- weight loss
- fatigue, headaches, irritability, depression
- anaemia (due to iron or folate deficiency)
- bone or joint pain; muscle cramps
- weakened bones (osteopaenia and osteoporosis) and teeth (loss of tooth enamel and colour)
- menstrual and pregnancy problems in women (missed periods; recurrent miscarriage)
- infertility in men and women
- delayed or stunted growth in infants and children
- pale sores inside the mouth, called aphthous ulcers
- itchy skin rash called dermatitis herpetiformis (DH)

What Causes Coeliac Disease?

The reason why some people's immune system reacts to gluten is not yet known, but genetic factors play a major role as the disease runs in families. Approximately 10% of people with an immediate family member with coeliac disease also have the condition. Environmental and lifestyle factors also play a role, as coeliac disease may only become active for the first time after a person experiences a period of physical or emotional stress, such as pregnancy, childbirth, surgery, intense emotional distress or a viral infection.

How Common Is Coeliac Disease?

For many years, coeliac disease was thought to be a relatively uncommon condition that mainly affected Caucasian people. However, recent studies have indicated that up to 1% of the population in Western countries may have coeliac disease (the prevalence has varied between studies from 1 in 100 people to 1 in 500 people); many of these people remain undiagnosed. Coeliac disease also appears to be more common in Africa, South America and Asia than previously believed, but the disease is most prevalent among people of European descent, particularly among the Irish. Approximately 5% of people with Type 1 diabetes also have coeliac disease and 5–10% of people with Down's syndrome also have coeliac disease.

What Are The Symptoms Of Coeliac Disease?

One reason why coeliac disease can be difficult to diagnose is that the condition affects people differently. For example, one person might have severe abdominal pain and chronic diarrhoea after eating, while another may feel irritable and tired, and a third may not experience any noticeable symptoms at all. Both the type and onset of symptoms varies among people with coeliac disease. Some people first develop symptoms as infants, whereas others don't experience symptoms until they are much older (teenage or adult age). Reasons why the disease is thought to affect people differently include the length of time they were breast-fed (in general, it appears that the longer a person was breast-fed as a baby, the longer it takes for their symptoms to develop); the age a person first started eating gluten-containing foods; the amount of gluten in their diet; and differences in the body's sensitivity to gluten.

Recent research has shown that the severity of symptoms experienced does not always reflect the amount of intestinal damage present, that is, people with greater damage do not always have the worst symptoms. People without symptoms will still suffer intestinal damage when they eat gluten and are still at risk of developing nutrient deficiencies and other complications. The longer a person with coeliac disease goes undiagnosed and untreated, the greater their chance of developing nutrient deficiencies and other complications. A prompt diagnosis is particularly important in children, because poor nutrition can cause serious developmental problems, such as growth, behavioural and learning difficulties.

What Health Problems Can Be Caused By Coeliac Disease?

The damaged small intestine in people with untreated coeliac disease has a reduced ability to absorb water and nutrients from digested food. Consequently, people with coeliac disease can experience abdominal bloating and painful cramps after eating a meal containing gluten. Unabsorbed food matter passes from the small into the large intestine, and can result in diarrhoea, large smelly stools or constipation. Increased flatulence (an increased amount of smelly gas) is also a common problem because bacteria that are naturally present in the large intestine can ferment fibre and starch in the unabsorbed food matter. The impaired food absorption can also result in various nutrient deficiencies. Due to decreased iron, folate and vitamin B12 absorption, people with untreated coeliac disease can develop complex anaemia, which makes them feel tired and possibly also irritable and depressed. People with a severely damaged small intestine may not absorb fat, fat-soluble vitamins (vitamins A, D, E and K), zinc or protein properly, resulting in weight loss, impaired growth in children, fatigue, miscarriages, infertility and other problems. Due to decreased calcium absorption, people with coeliac disease have an increased risk of osteopaenia and osteoporosis (weakened bones that are more susceptible to breaking). Lactose intolerance is also common in people with undiagnosed and newly diagnosed coeliac disease. This is because the damaged gut is unable to break down lactose—the sugar in cow's milk—which leads to symptoms such as abdominal bloating and pain after milk or certain dairy products are consumed.

People with untreated coeliac disease also have a small increased risk of intestinal cancer (lymphoma and adenocarcinoma), but this risk is reduced (to the same level as that for people without coeliac disease) after 3–5 years on a gluten-free diet. A nutritious gluten-free diet is essential for treating coeliac disease and for preventing or correcting the health problems caused by the condition.

What Diseases Are Linked To Coeliac Disease?

Due to unknown reasons (most likely genetic and environmental), people with coeliac disease have an increased risk of other autoimmune diseases including Type 1 diabetes, hypothyroidism (an under-active thyroid), systemic lupus erythematosus (Lupus), liver disease and rheumatoid arthritis.

How is Coeliac Disease Diagnosed?

It can be difficult for doctors to diagnose coeliac disease because the symptoms can be vague, or similar to those of other diseases, such as irritable bowel syndrome, Crohn's disease, diverticulitis, intestinal infections, iron-deficiency anaemia (due to increased blood loss or an inadequate iron intake) and chronic fatigue syndrome. Doctors may perform tests to rule out these conditions before they consider the possibility of coeliac disease. Consequently, it can take months or years before a person is properly diagnosed with coeliac disease. However, increased education and better diagnostic tests will make it easier for doctors to diagnose coeliac disease in the future. Coeliac organizations in many countries run educational campaigns to try to increase health professionals' awareness of the condition. You should definitely inform your doctor if you have a family history of coeliac disease, particularly if you also suffer from any of the associated symptoms.

At the moment, a biopsy of the small intestine is necessary to diagnose coeliac disease because the blood test to check for endomysial antibodies (EMA) and/or tissue transglutaminase antibodies (tTGA) is not perfect. People without coeliac disease can sometimes have high levels of the antibodies in their blood sample (a false positive result) and people with the condition can sometimes have low levels of antibodies (a false negative result).

What Happens Prior To Diagnosis?

If you think that you may have coeliac disease, it's important that you keep eating gluten-containing foods, such as regular bread, breakfast cereals and pasta, until you have been diagnosed with coeliac disease via a biopsy. If you stop eating gluten before being tested, your blood test and biopsy may be artificially negative for coeliac disease even if you do have the condition (it's just not apparent at that time because you have removed gluten from your diet). If you have adopted a gluten-free diet before

The diagnosis of coeliac disease generally occurs in three steps:

1. The first step is to discuss your concerns and symptoms with your doctor.
2. If your doctor suspects coeliac disease, you will need to have a blood test to check for the presence of endomysial antibodies (EMA) and/or tissue transglutaminase antibodies (tTGA). These antibodies tend to be present in higher levels in people with coeliac disease.
3. If your doctor feels that there is a chance that you have coeliac disease on the basis of your blood test and/or your symptoms, you will be referred to a gastroenterologist for a biopsy of your small intestine. To perform the biopsy, the gastroenterologist gradually eases a long flexible tube (endoscope) through your mouth down into your small intestine; this procedure is performed using local anaesthetic to minimise discomfort and patients often report that it wasn't as uncomfortable as they were expecting it to be. A tiny instrument is passed through the endoscope to collect a small tissue sample from your small intestine. The tissue sample is then taken to a lab and examined under a microscope. If the tissue abnormalities that occur with coeliac disease (inflammation and damaged villi) are found in the sample, the gastroenterologist or your doctor will inform you that you have coeliac disease.

being tested for coeliac disease, you will need to eat gluten-containing foods again for at least six weeks before undergoing the diagnostic tests. You may suffer some symptoms during this time, but your doctor won't be able to diagnose or rule out coeliac disease unless you have been eating gluten before the tests are performed.

What Is Dermatitis Herpetiformis?

Dermatitis herpetiformis (DH) is a non-contagious skin condition caused by gluten intolerance in genetically susceptible people. Some scientists consider it to be a type of coeliac disease, but not all people with coeliac disease have DH. DH affects fewer people than coeliac disease, approximately 1 in 10,000 people, and can appear at any age. DH results in red, raised blistering patches that are intensely itchy and sting when scratched. These patches can flare and subside, even if a person is not being treated, and often leave behind pale or brown areas of skin. DH can also result in a hive-like scaly rash, usually on the elbows, knees and buttocks, although it can affect any area of skin. People with DH may not have any gastrointestinal symptoms when they eat gluten, but they usually have some gut inflammation. Both the skin disease and any intestinal damage improve with a gluten-free diet. The itchy rash can also be controlled with medications.

What's the difference between coeliac disease and wheat allergy or intolerance?

People with coeliac disease have a permanent life-long intolerance to gluten and they need to maintain a gluten-free diet throughout their life in order to avoid intestinal damage and its associated complications. People with coeliac disease need to avoid all sources of gluten, not only wheat. In contrast, people with wheat allergy have an immune reaction to wheat protein, which quickly results in symptoms, such as swelling around the mouth, hives, rashes and eczema. Wheat allergy usually develops in young children and disappears as they get older but, in some rare cases, it can stay with a person for life. People with wheat allergy need only avoid foods that contain wheat and ingredients that contain the offending wheat protein. A wheat-free diet is less restrictive than a gluten-free diet. However, not all gluten-free foods are suitable for people with a wheat allergy because they may still contain some gluten-free sources of wheat protein, such as gluten-free wheat starch. Although rare, some people have a less severe intolerance to gluten, called non-coeliac gluten intolerance. Gluten consumption causes adverse symptoms in these people, such as nausea, diarrhoea, abdominal pain and bloating, but it doesn't cause the intestinal damage seen in coeliac disease. Most people with this type of gluten intolerance can tolerate small amounts of gluten (unlike people with coeliac disease).

To diagnose DH, a doctor will collect a blood sample to check for EMA and tTGA antibodies (the same as those tested when checking for coeliac disease) and a dermatologist (a specialist skin doctor) will take a small skin sample which will be checked for the presence of the antibody immunoglobulin A (IgA). An intestinal biopsy may also be required if the blood and skin tests are not definitive for DH.

What's The Treatment For Coeliac Disease And DH?

The only treatment for coeliac disease and DH is to follow a gluten-free diet for life. Eating any gluten, no matter how small an amount, can damage the small intestine in people with coeliac disease, even if they don't suffer any noticeable symptoms. Similarly, even tiny amounts of gluten can cause DH to flare up again and stop the skin from healing.

One of the best things you can do to learn about your new dietary requirements is to join your local coeliac disease or DH support organization. To find these, search the internet or your phone directory or ask your doctor for contact information. These organizations can provide you with excellent practical information about how to best manage your condition and where to find gluten-free foods. They often offer a lot of support for its members, including supermarket tours, educational talks, regular magazines and referral to expert dietitians. It's essential that you find an experienced dietitian to help you learn how you can identify gluten-free foods and correct any nutritional deficiencies you may have developed while your condition was undiagnosed. If you care for someone with coeliac disease or DH, such as a child or elderly relative, then you should also attend any dietary consultations and join your local coeliac organization for valuable support and education.

After starting a gluten-free diet, most people with coeliac disease quickly feel much better, though for other people the symptoms can linger. In people with DH, it may

Sources of gluten

Major sources
barley, barley flour, couscous, graham flour, kamut, rye, rye flour, semolina, spelt, triticale, wheat (atta, burghul/bulgar, bran, flour, germ, meal, farina) and foods based on wheat flour or flaked or puffed wheat (e.g. durum wheat pasta, noodles, cookies, bread, breakfast cereals, cakes, crackers, crumpets, muffins, rusks, scones, sauces)

Minor sources
cornflour (cornstarch), dextrin (postage stamp adhesive), malt, malted drink powders, malt extract, malt or grain vinegar, maltodextrin, modified starch, oats (bran, gum, flour, pilcorn, rolled, meal, scotch), pre-gel starch, starch, wheat starch, wheaten cornflour (cornstarch), some wheat-starch based thickeners

take 6 months or more for skin problems to disappear. However, as soon as you remove gluten from your diet, your gut and skin can start to heal. The small intestine is usually completely healed and able to absorb nutrients properly within 3–6 months in children and younger adults and within 2 years for older adults.

What Do I Do If My Symptoms Don't Improve?

Although it's rare, some people with coeliac disease show no improvement in their symptoms after adopting a gluten-free diet. Their condition is called unresponsive coeliac disease and requires treatment with a gluten-free diet and certain medications. However, the most common reason for a poor response is that small amounts of gluten are still being eaten. Unless you become skilled at reading food labels, you may inadvertently choose gluten-containing foods when shopping. Advice from an experienced dietitian is essential for helping you achieve a gluten-free diet that also meets your other nutritional needs. Your local coeliac organization can refer you to an expert dietitian in your area. You may need to see a dietitian frequently during the first few months after you've been diagnosed, but once you've begun mastering your new diet, you will be able to see them less often. After this, it's still worth consulting your dietitian every 6–12 months (or more often if you still have symptoms or other nutrition-related problems) for a dietary check-up.

What Is A Gluten-Free Diet?

A gluten-free diet means not eating foods that contain wheat (including spelt, triticale and kamut), rye, barley or oats or ingredients derived from these grains. Although this rules out a lot of foods, such as many types of bread, breakfast cereals, biscuits and pasta, there are many gluten-free versions of these foods available at supermarkets, health-food stores and from specialist food companies. In addition to gluten-free processed foods, there are also plenty of naturally gluten-free foods available, such as fruit, vegetables, legumes, meat, fish, eggs and nuts. So, it's definitely possible to have a nutritious, balanced gluten-free diet. Rather than thinking about all of the foods you can't have, focus on enjoying all of the foods you can eat. Some people find that the diagnosis of coeliac disease makes them improve the quality of their diet and their cooking skills, because they no longer rely on processed foods. It's also a great incentive to explore the huge variety of foods available, many of which you may never have eaten before, such as quinoa and buckwheat.

Gluten-free options

amaranth, arrowroot, besan (chickpea flour), buckwheat, buckwheat flour, cassava, cassava flour, corn/maize, cornmeal (polenta), gluten-free flour mixes, legumes, lentil flour, lotus root flour, lupin, maize cornflour (cornstarch) (without any added wheat flour/starch), millet, modified maize starch, potatoes, potato flour, potato starch, psyllium, quinoa, rice, rice bran, rice flour, baby rice cereal, sago, sorghum, soy flour, tapioca, tapioca flour, teff, vinegar (balsamic or wine), xanthan gum

Food ingredients with no detectable gluten*

caramel colour, dextrose, glucose, glucose powder, glucose syrup, wheat glucose syrup

* Even if derived from wheat.

Become A Gluten Detective: Look For Hidden Gluten In Processed Foods

A really important tool for maintaining a gluten-free diet is thoroughly reading the information on food labels. Gluten-containing ingredients are present in many processed foods and different brands of the same product can vary in their gluten content (for example, one brand of fish sauce contains gluten, whereas another brand doesn't). A qualified dietitian can help you learn how to interpret the information on food labels, and your local coeliac organization can provide you with information about gluten-free products and ingredients in your country. After a while, scanning food labels will become second nature to you and less time-consuming (initially you may need to take a list or handbook with you, if you can't remember all of the gluten-containing ingredients you need to check for). Many food companies also have lists or information about their gluten-free products that you can access via their website or by contacting the company's consumer service department (contact numbers are often listed on food labels and on websites). Some food companies refrain from adding a gluten-free label to a product, even if it really is gluten-free, because the product may not be gluten-free in the future if the company changes one of the ingredients.

Recent improvements to the food labelling laws in some countries have made it much easier for people to find gluten-free foods. All ingredients derived from gluten-containing grains must be declared in the ingredient list on food labels (for example, manufacturers have to list wheat starch rather than just starch). Products that have the words 'gluten-free' on their packaging must not contain any detectable gluten, oats or malt. There is also a crossed grain symbol that appears on some gluten-free foods in various countries to let you know that the product has been confirmed to be gluten-free. However, not all gluten-free foods carry this symbol and the food labelling laws differ between various countries.

When possible, always choose a product that has the words 'gluten-free' written on the label because some products that you would expect to be free of gluten, such as biscuits (cookies) made from rice flour, may be produced in a factory that also makes gluten-containing foods, such as biscuits made from wheat flour. Unless the manufacturer uses separate equipment to make the products and stores the ingredients separately, it is possible for cross-contamination to occur (for example, some wheat flour (gluten) ends up in the rice flour biscuit). Some specialist food companies are well aware of the potential for cross-contamination and maintain very strict manufacturing conditions to ensure that their gluten-free products are exactly that. However, not all companies are so aware of the problems of cross-contamination. It's also important to remember that 'wheat-free' products may not necessarily be free of gluten, so always check the ingredient list for any sources of gluten before purchasing wheat-free foods.

Gluten can also be found in medicines and nutrient supplements, so ask your doctor and pharmacist to check whether there is a gluten-free version of any medication or supplement you are advised to take. The adhesive on postage stamps and envelopes may also contain gluten. So look for non-lickable stamps and envelopes or moisten stamps and envelopes with a wet sponge.

Products that may contain gluten – always check the ingredient list

baking powder
cheese flavour
cheese spread
chutney
coffee whitener
compound chocolate
confectionery
cornflakes
corn tortillas
curry sauces/mixes/powder
dill pickles and gherkins
drink mixes
dry-roasted nuts
flavoured potato chips (crisps)
frozen chips (fries)
grated cheese (pre-grated)

gravy mixes
instant dried mashed potato
lecithin
mayonnaise
mustard
pickles
poppadoms
processed meats
puffed corn cereal
puffed rice cakes (mixed grain
   varieties are also available)
puffed rice cereal
relish
salad dressings
salami
sauces (e.g. fish, hoisin,

oyster, pasta, tomato,
soy, sichuan, tamari,
worcestershire)
sauce mixes
sausages
seasoning mixes
soba noodles
soft drinks (cloudy-style)
soup (tinned and dried)
soy milk and soy yoghurt
stock (ready-made, cubes or
   powder)
white pepper (flour may be added
   for extra bulk)
yeast
yoghurt

Tips For Eating A Balanced, Nutritious Gluten-Free Diet

General healthy eating guidelines for people with coeliac disease and DH are the same as those for people without these conditions—with the exception that all foods must be gluten-free and any nutrient deficiencies present after diagnosis are corrected through the sensible use of supplements together with healthy eating (supplement use should be guided by your doctor and dietitian):

1. Eat a wide variety of nutritious foods each day

Most of the food you eat each day should be fruit, vegetables (including fresh herbs), legumes and gluten-free cereal products, such as rice and other gluten-free grains, gluten-free bread, pasta and breakfast cereals. If you also have diabetes, you should choose low-GI versions of these foods, such as basmati rice, wild rice, quinoa, corn, sweet potato and temperate fruit. Try to eat a variety of different coloured fruits and vegetables each week. Green vegetables and fresh herbs are excellent sources of folate and various antioxidants, and should be eaten daily.

2. Watch your fat intake

When the villi recover, the intestine is able to absorb more nutrients and some people will start to gain weight. This may be desirable for children and adults who have lost weight, but it's important to keep your weight within the healthy weight range. If you need to control your weight, it's important that you don't eat more fat than you need. You can do this by switching to lower-fat dairy products, choosing lean cuts of meat and skinless poultry, using low-fat cooking methods, and minimizing your intake of fatty foods and added fats, such as mayonnaise, oily salad dressings, butter, cream and margarine. Aim to eat nutritious foods as snacks rather than less nutritious 'junk' foods as these will help top up your body's nutrient stores. For example, choose fresh fruit or cheese on gluten-free bread instead of potato chips or confectionery.

Improve the quality of fat in your diet by making monounsaturated and omega-3 polyunsaturated fat the main fats in your diet. Unlike saturated fat, these fats help protect against heart disease and Type 2 diabetes. Increasing your omega-3 fat intake can also help reduce inflammation, which may in turn help your villi heal faster. Good sources of monounsaturated fat include avocados, olives, olive oil (preferably extra virgin), canola oil and most nuts. Good sources of omega-3 polyunsaturated fat include oily fish, such as salmon, tuna, mackerel, trout, sardines, herrings, blue eye and

redfish; omega-3-enriched eggs, walnuts, linseeds (flax seeds) and canola oil. Aim to include fish in your diet 3–4 times a week. The main oils you cook with should be olive and canola oil and if you eat margarine or mayonnaise, use a lower fat variety based on olive or canola oil.

3. Eat moderate amounts of protein-rich foods

Red meat, poultry, eggs, liver, fish and seafood all provide good amounts of protein, iron, zinc and vitamin B12. If you have had undiagnosed coeliac disease for some time, you may not have been absorbing adequate amounts of these nutrients. If so, ask your doctor to perform a blood test to check whether you are deficient in iron, folate or vitamin B12. You may initially require some nutrient supplements to build up your body's stores, particularly if you're vegetarian. Try to include rich sources of these nutrients in your diet on a regular basis (for example, red meat at least 3–4 times a week). Stir-fries are a great way to include meat, poultry, fish or seafood in your diet together with a variety of vegetables, and are delicious served with rice or gluten-free rice noodles. Vegetarian sources of protein, such as legumes, tofu and grain-based foods, do not provide as much iron or zinc as animal foods. If you're vegetarian, it is important to consult a dietitian for advice on how to maximize the amount of iron and zinc you absorb from your meals.

4. Regularly eat good sources of calcium

Including calcium-rich foods in your daily diet is essential for reducing the risk of osteoporosis. Dairy foods are the best sources of calcium available because lactose— milk sugar—enhances calcium absorption in our body. Three serves of dairy products a day generally meet most people's calcium requirements (a cup of milk; 200 g (7 oz) yoghurt; a wedge of cheese). However, some people with undiagnosed or newly diagnosed coeliac disease will also be lactose intolerant due to their damaged small intestine. The lactose intolerance often disappears when the gut has healed after a period of gluten-free eating. Lactose intolerant people can choose calcium-enriched alternatives, such as gluten-free soy milk and lactose-free cow's milk, but they may

Recommended foods* (or gluten-free versions)

Cereal Products (grains, flours)
- Gluten-free bread, pasta, and breakfast cereals
- Porridge made from soy or rice flakes
- Gluten-free snack bars
- Noodles—rice, mung bean, buckwheat*
- Puffed rice and corn cakes*
- Gluten-free rice crackers and biscuits
- Rice, millet, quinoa, buckwheat, sorghum, teff, cornmeal (cornstarch), sago, tapioca, rice bran, baby rice cereal
- Gluten-free corn tortillas and taco shells
- Rice paper, gluten-free lasagne or rice noodle sheets

Fruit and Vegetables
- Fresh fruit and fruit juices
- Dried fruit* and glacé fruit*
- Fresh vegetables and fresh vegetable juice
- Plain vegetables—frozen, dried, tinned and bottled*

Legumes
- Dried legumes (soaked and freshly boiled)
- Plain, tinned legumes*
- Legume flours (e.g. chickpea flour, lentil flour)

Dairy products and alternatives
- Cow's milk
- Cream, butter, sour cream
- Condensed milk*
- Coconut milk
- Gluten-free yoghurts and fromage frais
- Aged cheese and soft cheese*
- Gluten-free soy milk (no malt or maltodextrin)
- Plain ice cream
- Tofu
- Rice milk

Beverages
- Water—tap, spring, mineral, soda, tonic
- Tea, coffee
- Soft drinks*
- Fruit juice
- Wine, liqueurs, spirits
- Carob powder and pure unsweetened cocoa powder

Spreads and condiments
- Jam and pure fruit spreads
- Honey, golden syrup, maple syrup
- Peanut butter
- Vinegar—balsamic and wine
- Lemon juice, lime juice
- Gluten-free tamari
- Tomato paste (concentrated purée)*
- Tahini

Foods to avoid

- Bread containing wheat, rye, triticale, oats or barley (or any other gluten-containing ingredient)
- Muesli or breakfast cereals with gluten-containing grains, malt flavourings or malt extract
- Muesli bars, breakfast cereal snack bars
- Durum wheat pasta and wheat flour noodles (e.g. instant, udon, hokkien)
- Rolled oats, oat-based porridge, oat bran, oat meal
- Wheat bran, wheat germ, wheat meal
- Couscous
- Semolina

- Some commercial fruit pie fillings
- Some snack foods with fruit fillings
- Battered vegetables and fritters
- Some brands of frozen French fries/chips
- Textured vegetable protein
- Tinned vegetables in sauce*

- Tinned baked beans*
- Convenience vegetarian meals*

- Malted milk and some flavoured milk
- Cheese spreads*
- Ice cream in a cone
- Custard* and custard powder
- Flavoured ice cream*
- Some flavoured yoghurts and dairy desserts
- Oat milk

- Drinking chocolate and drink mixes*
- Coffee substitutes
- Lemon barley water
- Malted milk drinks
- Beer, lager, ale, stout, Guinness

- Yeast extract spreads – vegemite, marmite, promite
- Soy sauce*
- Commercial chutneys, relishes and pickles*
- Malt vinegar
- Commercial salad dressings* and mayonnaise*
- Many commercial sauces; different brands of the same sauce may vary in their gluten content

* Check the product's ingredient list. Individual brands may vary in their gluten content.

also require a calcium supplement. Some people who have had long-standing untreated coeliac disease and/or a low calcium intake may also require a calcium supplement to help boost their body's stores. Ask your doctor or dietitian for advice about whether a calcium supplement is suitable for you.

5. Include good sources of fibre in your daily diet

Relying on commercial gluten-free breads, pasta, biscuits and cereals can decrease your fibre intake, because many of these commercial varieties are based on corn and

Products to include in a gluten-free kitchen

Pantry

gluten-free flours: white rice, potato, chickpea, tapioca (store in opaque containers)

commercial gluten-free flour mixtures: plain/all-purpose, self-raising, bread mix

grains: arrowroot, polenta, quinoa, buckwheat, rice, wild rice, sago, tapioca

gluten-free processed foods: bread, breakfast cereals, biscuits, snack bars and pasta

noodles: dried rice noodles, mung bean noodles

nuts and seeds: linseeds (flax seeds), sunflower seeds, sesame seeds and raw nuts

dried legumes and gluten-free tinned varieties: chickpeas, cannellini beans, kidney beans, lentils and split peas

fruit: gluten-free dried fruit and tinned fruit

drinks: coffee and tea

baking ingredients: gluten-free baking powder, baking soda, pure spices, gelatine, natural vanilla extract, xanthan gum, guar gum and psyllium fibre

sweeteners: sugar, pure icing (confectioners') sugar, pure unsweetened cocoa powder, carob powder

milk products: UHT milk, condensed milk, dried milk powder, tinned coconut milk

oils: extra virgin olive oil, olive oil and canola oil

snacks or serving suggestions: gluten-free taco shells, plain popping corn, plain gluten-free poppadoms

tinned fish

gluten-free sauces: tamari, fish, soy, tomato and pasta

Refrigerator

milk: cow's, rice drink or gluten-free soy milk

fats: butter or margarine

eggs

dairy products: gluten-free cheese, yoghurt, fromage frais and sour cream

spreads: pure fruit jam, peanut butter, honey and tahini

drinks: fruit juice, mineral water and spring water

corn tortillas

meat: low-fat gluten-free processed meats and bacon slices

seeds and flours: ground linseeds (flax seeds), soy flour and brown rice flour (these keep for longer when stored in the refrigerator)

fruit and vegetables

Freezer

gluten-free bread products: bread and breadcrumbs (fresh and dry)

gluten-free baked goods: muffins and corn tortillas,

stock: home-made gluten-free stock and meals (freeze single portions to reheat when you're too busy to cook)

gluten-free low-fat ice cream

gluten-free frozen yoghurt

gluten-free yeast (this keeps better in the freezer)

frozen vegetables: spinach, peas, corn, broccoli, cauliflower and stir-fry mixtures rice flour. These flours contain less fibre than wheat flour. Fibre-rich foods are important for preventing constipation and other bowel problems. Good gluten-free sources of fibre include linseed (flax) meal (you can add this to breakfast cereal, yoghurt or baked goods), sunflower seeds (these can be added to salads), brown rice, buckwheat, quinoa, legumes, nuts and fresh vegetables and fruit. And remember to drink water throughout the day—this also helps keep you regular.

6. Drink gluten-free alcohol in moderation

If you drink alcohol, enjoy it in moderation. This means several alcohol-free days each week and 4 or fewer standard drinks for males and 2 or fewer standard drinks for females on any one day. In fact, it may be helpful to avoid alcohol entirely during the first few months after being diagnosed with coeliac disease in order to help your gut heal and absorb nutrients properly. Wine, spirits and liqueurs are typically gluten-free. Beer, stout, ale, Guinness and lager should all be avoided because they contain gluten.

What Are The Challenges of Gluten-Free Baking?

Gluten provides the strength and elasticity that helps hold bakery products together. It also helps bakery products rise and obtain a light aerated texture on the inside and a crumbed texture on the surface. Consequently, gluten-free flours don't always produce the same results when substituted for wheat flour. Fortunately, many people have been experimenting with gluten-free baking methods for some time, so you can benefit from the results of their experiments.

Tips For Successful Gluten-Free Baking

• In baking, a mixture of flours works best. This is why many commercial gluten-free flour mixtures contain a number of different flours.

• It's helpful to add some guar gum, xanthan gum or gluten-free pre-gel starch to gluten-free flour mixtures because they mimic the properties of gluten and help reduce crumbling in baked goods. You can get these gums from health-food stores,

Make your own flour mixes

Plain (all-purpose) flour
1. Mix 6 parts rice flour with 2 parts potato flour and 1 part tapioca flour.
2. Mix 2 parts soy flour with 1 part rice flour and 1 part potato flour.
3. Use 1 part each of soy flour and potato flour; soy flour and rice flour; or soy flour and maize cornflour (cornstarch).
4. Use 4 parts soy flour, 4 parts potato flour, 1 part rice flour, and 1 part glutinous rice flour.

Self-raising flour
Put 2 tablespoons potato flour into a measuring cup, then add sufficient white rice flour to bring the total volume of the mixture to 1 cup. Sift the mixture into a bowl and add ½ teaspoon bicarbonate of soda (baking soda), ½ teaspoon cream of tartar, and 1 teaspoon xanthan gum (or guar gum).

Baking powder
Mix together 1 part bicarbonate of soda (baking soda) and 2 parts cream of tartar.

specialist food stores and some coeliac organizations. For cakes, add ¼ teaspoon gum per 150 g (5½ oz/1 cup) of gluten-free flour; for breads, add 1 teaspoon gum per 150 g (5½ oz/1 cup) of flour; for pizza crusts, add 2 teaspoons gum per 150 g (5½ oz/1 cup) of flour. Gluten-free gluten substitute is another new ingredient that you can experiment with.

• You can make your own gluten-free flour mixture and gluten-free baking powder (see box on left). Sift the flours together three times before using, then substitute by weight, not by volume, when converting recipes.

• If you find the taste of regular soy flour a little unpleasant, use debittered soy flour.

• You may achieve better results by increasing the amount of baking powder in cake mixes and by adding an additional egg to gluten-free pancake batters.

• Gluten-free pastry or biscuit (cookie) dough is easier to work with if you refrigerate it for 30 minutes before forming into biscuits.

• Apple sauce can be used instead of oil in baking to add extra moisture (while reducing fat) to gluten-free waffles, cakes and pancakes (although you may need to experiment the first few times).

• Adding extra eggs, milk powder or soy flour can help to produce a less crumbly texture in gluten-free breads and cakes.

• Gluten-free bread dough often has a batter-like consistency, which means it can't be kneaded and shaped as easily as wheat-flour based bread doughs. However, you can easily make gluten-free bread rolls by using pie tins or muffin tins or you can shape moulds out of aluminium foil and place them on a baking tray

• Make sure you store gluten-free flours separately from gluten-containing flours, in labelled containers, to avoid cross-contamination. Brown rice flour and soy flour should be stored in the refrigerator, whereas other gluten-free flours can be stored in a cool dark place. For long-term storage, keep gluten-free flours in the freezer in well-sealed containers. Gluten-free yeast should also be stored in the freezer.

• Gluten-free bakery products may not keep their freshness as long as regular versions. You can freeze wrapped individual portions of gluten-free bakery goods so you can enjoy them later on.

• Using heavy-duty tins for baking, rather than aluminium ones, will help gluten-free cakes and breads cook evenly so that the centre is cooked at the same time as the outside, rather than having a soggy centre and a hard crust. Test your tins with a magnet—if the magnet sticks to the tin, it's fine to use. Ring-shaped tins are particularly good for cakes. To prevent the dough from sticking to the tin, grease the cooking tin before adding the dough or line it with baking paper.

• To produce a good gluten-free bakery product, you need the right ingredients and the right oven temperature. Sometimes gluten-free baked goods don't work because the oven is not working properly. You can check whether your oven is working properly by using an oven thermometer, which can be purchased from a good kitchenware shop (or over the internet).

Eating well with gluten intolerance

• Keep your pantry, refrigerator and freezer well stocked with gluten-free foods, so you always have something suitable on hand when you need it.

• If you have a busy lifestyle, cook double portions of meals, so you can freeze the leftovers.

• Take suitable foods with you to work or school, to the movies, while out shopping or travelling

• Take suitable gluten-free foods with you to parties and social events.

• Contact your local coeliac organization to find out about restaurants and cafés in your area that cater for people on gluten-free diets.

• If you're in doubt about a menu item, ask the waiter or chef about the ingredients and preparation methods or ask if a gluten-free option is available.

• If some people in your family eat regular foods and others require gluten-free foods, make sure you store the two types of foods separately to avoid cross-contamination. You may need to designate a special shelf in the pantry for gluten-free foods only, so gluten-containing foods are not grabbed by mistake. Use separate cutting boards and knives for gluten-free and regular bread, and use separate toasters (or shake out the crumbs thoroughly between toasting gluten-free bread) to make sure that gluten-free bread is not contaminated. You may also need to have separate containers of margarine, butter and spreads, so gluten-containing breadcrumbs are not eaten by family members who need to follow a gluten-free diet.

• If you have a child who requires a gluten-free diet, speak with their teachers about their condition and dietary requirements. Your child's friends and their parents should also be informed.

- Gluten-free breads can sink after being taken out of an oven if the kitchen is too humid or if the bread was left to rise too long before being placed in the oven. If you make a yeast-leavened dough that doesn't rise properly, make it again and add 1 teaspoon of vinegar or a pinch of citric acid to the water before you add the yeast.
- Make your own gluten-free dried breadcrumbs by placing gluten-free bread slices in a slow oven to dry (the bread should turn a golden colour), then put the dried bread in a food processor or crush using a rolling pin. The breadcrumbs can be stored in the freezer for several months.
- Commercial gluten-free bread mixes can be used to make pizza bases (don't let the dough rise), pikelets and pancakes.
- Remember that no matter how much you experiment, some bakery products just won't work when made with gluten-free flour. However, there are plenty of other delicious gluten-free recipes you can try instead.

How to use this book

All the recipes in this book are free of gluten. For ingredients that typically contain gluten (such as flour, bread and cereals) we have specified that you choose a gluten-free version. For ingredients that occasionally contain gluten we have used the symbol GF so you know to check the ingredient list.

The nutritional analysis of recipes does not include any serving suggestions or garnishes.

Disclaimer

The information in this book is intended to provide people with coeliac disease and/or dermatitis herpetiformis (DH), and people who care for them, with general advice about healthy gluten-free eating (accurate at the time of printing). This advice may not be sufficient for some people with multiple health problems or serious complications. It is not intended to replace any advice given to you by a qualified doctor or other mainstream health professional. It is important that both coeliac disease and DH are diagnosed by a doctor, using standard diagnostic tests (blood samples, biopsies and assessment of your symptoms). Neither the author nor the publishers can be held responsible for claims arising from the inappropriate use or incorrect interpretation of any of the dietary advice described in this book.

BREAKFAST

ROLLED RICE PORRIDGE

WHO DOESN'T LOVE PORRIDGE ON A COLD WINTER'S MORNING? USING THIS RECIPE, YOU CAN ENJOY A WARM NOURISHING PORRIDGE THAT'S FREE OF GLUTEN. TRY IT WITH A VARIETY OF TOPPINGS.

**50 g (1¾ oz/½ cup) rolled rice or
  rice flakes
pure maple syrup, to serve
fresh fruit, to serve
milk, to serve**

PREP TIME: 5 MINUTES
COOKING TIME: 20 MINUTES
SERVES 1

Combine the rolled rice or rice flakes and 500 ml (17 fl oz/2 cups) boiling water in a saucepan. Cover with a lid and simmer over medium heat for 20 minutes, or until soft and creamy. Serve topped with maple syrup, fresh fruit and milk.

HINTS:
• If you'd like a sweeter porridge, try replacing a little of the water with fruit juice. You'll need to bring it to a boil before using it.
• If you have diabetes, it's best to avoid this meal or enjoy it as an occasional treat, because it is a high-GI meal (meaning it will cause a high blood-sugar response). Use soy flakes instead of rice flakes to produce a lower GI porridge.
• Try other toppings, such as gluten-free dried fruit, rice bran, honey or soft brown sugar.

nutrition per serve: Energy 776 kJ (184 Cal); Fat 1.6 g; Saturated fat 0.4 g; Protein 4 g; Carbohydrate 39 g; Fibre 1.2 g; Cholesterol 0 mg

WHEAT-FREE MUESLI

MUESLI IS A GREAT WAY TO EAT A VARIETY OF HEALTHY FOODS IN JUST ONE BOWL. THE SEEDS AND NUTS ADD MINERALS, ANTIOXIDANTS AND FIBRE, MAKING THIS MUESLI NUTRITIOUS AND SUSTAINING.

90 g (3¼ oz/3 cups) gluten-free puffed corn (non-malted)
60 g (2¼ oz/2 cups) puffed rice GF
90 g (3¼ oz/1 cup) rice bran
100 g (3½ oz/1 cup) LSA mix
80 g (2¾ oz/½ cup) roasted unsalted macadamia nuts, chopped
70 g (2½ oz/½ cup) roasted hazelnuts, chopped
70 g (2½ oz/½ cup) pepitas (pumpkin seeds)

60 g (2¼ oz/½ cup) sunflower seeds
135 g (4¾ oz/1 cup) chopped mixed dried fruit, such as dried pears, peaches and apricots
fruit juice or milk, to serve
low-fat plain yoghurt, to serve

PREP TIME: 10 MINUTES
COOKING TIME: NIL
SERVES 10

Put the grains, nuts, seeds and dried fruit in a large bowl and stir together thoroughly. Store in an airtight container until ready to use.

When ready to serve, top with the fruit juice or milk and the yoghurt.

HINTS:
• LSA mix is a mixture of linseeds, sunflower seeds and almonds.
• To reduce the fat content of this recipe, omit the LSA mix or replace it with a little ground linseeds.
• If you would like to serve this with flavoured yoghurt, check the label to make sure that there are no gluten-containing ingredients.

nutrition per serve: Energy 1509 kJ (361 Cal); Fat 21.8 g; Saturated fat 2.4 g; Protein 8.9 g; Carbohydrate 25.9 g; Fibre 9.5 g; Cholesterol 0 mg

CITRUS SUMMER SALAD

3 ruby grapefruit
3 large oranges
1 tbsp caster (superfine) sugar
1 cinnamon stick
1 tbsp mint, chopped
whole mint leaves, to garnish
low-fat plain yoghurt, to serve

PREP TIME: 15 MINUTES
COOKING TIME: 5 MINUTES
SERVES 4–6

Peel and remove the pith from the grapefruit and oranges. Carefully cut out the segments and mix together in a bowl.

Put the sugar, cinnamon stick and mint in a small saucepan with 3 tablespoons water and stir over low heat until the sugar has dissolved.

Remove the cinnamon stick and strain the mint from the syrup, then drizzle the syrup over the fruit. Garnish with fresh mint leaves and serve with yoghurt.

HINTS:
- Another good combination for a citrus fruit salad is mandarins, tangelos and pomelos when they are in season. Add some pomegranate seeds for a burst of colour.
- This fruit salad can be kept, covered, in the refrigerator for up to 2 days and the flavour will improve over time.
- If you take prescription medication, check whether you can still eat grapefruit while taking this medication (ask your pharmacist or check the information sheet inside the medication pack). Grapefruit contains a compound that can interfere with the metabolism of certain medications. If you do take a prescription drug, you can simply swap the grapefruit with mandarins, tangelos or any other fruit of your choice.
- If you use flavoured yoghurt instead of plain, check the ingredient list to ensure the yoghurt is free of gluten.

THIS REFRESHING CITRUS FRUIT
SALAD WILL GIVE YOU A BOOST
OF ANTIOXIDANTS AND IS A GREAT
CHOICE WHEN YOU WANT A LIGHT
BUT HEALTHY MEAL. TOP IT WITH
SOME GLUTEN-FREE YOGHURT FOR
EXTRA PROTEIN AND CALCIUM. IT'S
ALSO GOOD AS A SNACK.

nutrition per serve (6)   Energy 315 kJ (75 Cal)
Fat 0.3 g
Saturated fat 0 g
Protein 2 g
Carbohydrate 15.6 g
Fibre 2.8 g
Cholesterol 0 mg

PANCAKES

YOU DON'T NEED TO MISS OUT ON DELICIOUS FOOD JUST BECAUSE YOU'RE ON A GLUTEN-FREE DIET. BY CHOOSING THE RIGHT INGREDIENTS, YOU CAN MAKE GLUTEN-FREE VERSIONS OF MANY POPULAR RECIPES, LIKE THESE PANCAKES.

190 g (6¾ oz/1¼ cups) gluten-free plain (all-purpose) flour
2 tsp gluten-free baking powder
1 egg
1 tbsp canola or olive oil
mixed berries, to serve
pure maple syrup, to serve

PREP TIME: 10 MINUTES
COOKING TIME: 20 MINUTES
MAKES 10

Sift the flour and baking powder into a bowl and make a well in the centre. Mix together the egg, oil and 310 ml (10¾ fl oz/1¼ cups) water, then add to the well in the dry ingredients. Stir until the batter is smooth and reaches the consistency of thin cream, adding up to another 3 tablespoons water if necessary. Strain the batter into a vessel with a pouring lip.

Lightly brush a 20 cm (8 in) frying pan with oil and heat over medium heat. Pour in just enough mixture to thinly cover the bottom of the pan. When the top of the pancake starts to set, use a spatula to turn it over. After browning the second side, transfer to a plate. Repeat with the remaining pancake batter, greasing the pan between each batch. Serve with berries and maple syrup.

HINTS:
• The pancake batter can be made the day before and stored in a covered container in the refrigerator—a great time saver in the morning.
• Pure maple syrup is concentrated from the sap of the maple tree. Do not confuse it with the cheaper maple-flavoured syrup, which is artificially coloured and flavoured and has a much higher GI value (so it will cause a high blood-sugar response).
• These pancakes go well with many different toppings, for example, pure fruit jam, lemon juice with sugar, and even gluten-free chocolate hazelnut spread.

nutrition per pancake: Energy 408 kJ (97 Cal); Fat 2.7 g; Saturated fat 0.4 g; Protein 0.9 g; Carbohydrate 17 g; Fibre 0.3 g; Cholesterol 19 mg

BUCKWHEAT PANCAKES

HERE'S ANOTHER DELICIOUS GLUTEN-FREE VERSION OF PANCAKES THAT THE WHOLE FAMILY WILL ENJOY. USE WHOLE KERNEL (GROAT) BUCKWHEAT FLOUR FOR EXTRA NUTRIENTS (FIBRE, PROTEIN, VITAMINS AND MINERALS).

135 g (4¾ oz/1 cup) buckwheat flour
1 egg
pure maple syrup, to serve

PREP TIME: 10 MINUTES
COOKING TIME: 20 MINUTES
MAKES 16–20

Sift the flour into a bowl and make a well in the centre. In a separate bowl mix the egg with 185 ml (6 fl oz/¾ cup) water, then pour into the well in the dry ingredients. Beat with a wooden spoon until the batter is combined and smooth. Pour the batter into a vessel with a pouring lip.

Brush a 20 cm (8 in) frying pan with oil and heat over medium heat. Pour in just enough batter to thinly cover the bottom of the pan.

When the top of the pancake starts to set, turn it over with a spatula. After browning the second side, transfer to a plate. Repeat with the remaining pancake batter, greasing the pan between batches. Serve with a drizzle of maple syrup.

HINTS:
* These pancakes are also delicious served with other toppings, such as pure fruit jam, fresh berries and gluten-free yoghurt—just to name a few.
* If you're watching your weight, use spray oil to grease the pan.
* If some members of your family eat gluten, make sure to store the gluten-free and gluten-containing products (especially flour) separately to avoid cross-contamination.

nutrition per pancake (20): Energy 118 kJ (28 Cal); Fat 0.7 g; Saturated fat 0.2 g; Protein 1.2 g; Carbohydrate 4.1 g; Fibre 0.7 g; Cholesterol 9 mg

SCRAMBLED EGGS ARE ONE OF
THE ALL-TIME CLASSIC BREAKFAST
MEALS. ADDING GRILLED
MUSHROOMS AND TOMATOES
MAKES THEM EVEN MORE
DELICIOUS AND NUTRITIOUS.

nutrition per serve Energy 2303 kJ (550 Cal)

Fat 29.3 g

Saturated fat 6.8 g

Protein 30.5 g

Carbohydrate 41.4 g

Fibre 7.1 g

Cholesterol 563 mg

SCRAMBLED EGGS WITH GRILLED TOMATOES AND MUSHROOMS

4 field mushrooms

2 vine-ripened tomatoes, halved

canola or olive oil spray

2 tsp thyme, plus extra to garnish

6 eggs

1 tbsp reduced-fat milk

30 g (1 oz) reduced-fat canola or olive oil
  margarine

4 slices of gluten-free bread, toasted

PREP TIME: 5 MINUTES

COOKING TIME: 10 MINUTES

SERVES 2

Put the mushrooms and tomatoes, cut side up, under a preheated grill (broiler), then spray with oil and scatter with the thyme leaves. Cook for 3–5 minutes, or until warmed.

Meanwhile, break the eggs into a bowl, add the milk and season well with salt and freshly ground black pepper. Whisk gently with a fork until well combined.

Melt half the margarine in a small non-stick saucepan or frying pan over low heat. Add the eggs, then stir constantly with a wooden spoon. Do not turn up the heat—scrambling must be done slowly and gently. When most of the egg has set, add the remaining margarine and remove the pan from the heat. There should be enough heat left in the pan to finish cooking the eggs and melt the margarine. Serve immediately on toast. Arrange the tomatoes and mushrooms on the side. Garnish with extra thyme leaves.

HINTS:
• For the best results, use fresh eggs when scrambling. To check whether an egg is fresh, put it in a bowl of cold water. If the egg sinks on its side it is fresh; if it floats on its end it is stale. If it is somewhere between the two it is not perfectly fresh but still good enough to use for scrambled eggs.
• If some members of your family eat gluten-containing bread, make sure to use separate toasters or shake out the crumbs before each use.

CRUMPETS

MANY PEOPLE THINK THAT A GLUTEN-FREE DIET MEANS GIVING UP BREAD
AND BAKERY PRODUCTS COMPLETELY. FORTUNATELY, THAT'S NOT TRUE. IF
YOU LOVE CRUMPETS, GIVE THIS RECIPE A TRY.

**450 g (1 lb/3 cups) gluten-free self-raising
    flour**
1 tbsp caster (superfine) sugar
1 tsp salt
2 tsp dried yeast GF
435 ml (15¼ fl oz/1¾ cups) lukewarm milk
½ tsp bicarbonate of soda (baking soda)
butter, to serve
strawberry jam GF **(Basics), to serve**

PREP TIME: 15 MINUTES +
    1¼ HOURS STANDING
COOKING TIME: 45 MINUTES
MAKES 10

Combine the flour, sugar, salt and yeast in a large bowl. Pour in the milk and whisk well to combine. Cover and set aside in a warm place for 1 hour, or until doubled in size.

Use a spoon to beat the mixture until it deflates. Combine 4 tablespoons lukewarm water and the bicarbonate of soda in a small bowl, then whisk into the batter until smooth. Set aside for 15 minutes.

Brush a large heavy-based non-stick frying pan with oil and heat over medium heat. Brush four 9.5 x 2 cm (3¾ x ¾ in) crumpet rings with oil, then place in the pan and reduce the heat to low. Pour enough batter into each crumpet ring to fill to three-quarters full. Cook for 12–15 minutes, or until large bubbles come to the surface, the base is golden and the top is set (if the bubbles don't pop you can use a skewer to pierce the holes). Cover the pan and cook for a further 2–3 minutes. Use a sharp knife to carefully loosen the crumpets and remove from the rings. Put the crumpets on a wire rack. Wash the crumpet rings and re-grease. Repeat with the remaining batter. Serve with butter and fruit jam.

HINTS:
• You can buy crumpet rings from some supermarkets and kitchenware shops.
• Each brand of commercial gluten-free flour mixture varies in the amount of different flours it contains. This means that some brands may work better with certain recipes than others, so be prepared to experiment. Check the flour's packaging to see if there is any information about the types of recipes that the flour mixture suits best.
• Gluten-free yeast should be stored in the freezer.

nutrition per serve: Energy 845 kJ (202 Cal); Fat 2.8 g; Saturated fat 1.2 g; Protein 3.7 g;
Carbohydrate 39 g; Fibre 3.8 g; Cholesterol 6 mg

WAFFLES

HERE'S ANOTHER SURPRISE—GLUTEN-FREE WAFFLES. YOU WILL NEED A WAFFLE IRON TO MAKE THESE AND YOU MAY NEED TO TRY DIFFERENT BRANDS OF GLUTEN-FREE FLOUR TO FIND THE ONE THAT GIVES THE BEST RESULT.

250 g (9 oz/2 cups) soy-containing, gluten-free self-raising flour
3 tbsp caster (superfine) sugar
300 ml (10½ fl oz) milk
2 eggs
60 g (2¼ oz) butter, melted, cooled
butter, to serve
strawberry jam GF (Basics), to serve

PREP TIME: 10 MINUTES +
15 MINUTES RESTING
COOKING TIME: 30 MINUTES
MAKES 6

To make the batter, sift the flour into a large bowl, stir in the sugar, then make a well in the centre. In a separate bowl, whisk the milk and eggs together. Pour the milk mixture into the well in the dry ingredients and whisk until smooth. Whisk in the melted butter. Set the batter aside to rest for 10–15 minutes.

Preheat a waffle maker. Pour ⅓-cupfuls (4 tablespoons) of the batter into the waffle maker and cook following the waffle maker's instructions. Transfer to a wire rack and repeat with the remaining batter, allowing the waffle maker to reheat between waffles. Serve the waffles with strawberry jam.

HINTS:
• It's important to use a gluten-free flour that contains soy flour when making these waffles. Soy flour acts more like gluten flour so gives a better result in some recipes. Check the ingredients list of the packet of flour.
• You can make these waffles with rice drink or gluten-free soy milk, if you can't use cow's milk; you'll need 300 ml (10½ fl oz).
• These waffles are great with a variety of toppings, such as pure maple syrup, golden syrup, honey or fruit jam. If you buy jam, check the label to ensure it is free of gluten.

nutrition per serve: Energy 1293 kJ (309 Cal); Fat 12.5 g; Saturated fat 5.3 g; Protein 7.2 g; Carbohydrate 40 g; Fibre 2.5 g; Cholesterol 82 mg

POACHED EGGS WITH SPINACH AND GARLIC YOGHURT DRESSING

DRESSING
125 g (4½ oz/½ cup) low-fat plain
    yoghurt
1 small garlic clove, crushed
1 tbsp snipped chives

300 g (10½ oz/6 cups) baby English
    spinach leaves
15 g (½ oz) butter

4 tomatoes, halved
1 tbsp white vinegar
8 eggs
8 thick slices of gluten-free bread, toasted

PREP TIME: 10 MINUTES
COOKING TIME: 15 MINUTES
SERVES 4

To make the dressing, mix together the yoghurt, garlic and chives.

Wash the spinach and put it in a large saucepan with just the little water that is left clinging to the leaves. Cover the pan and cook over low heat for 3–4 minutes, or until the spinach has wilted. Add the butter, then season with salt and freshly ground black pepper and toss together. Remove the pan from the heat and keep warm.

Put the tomatoes, cut side up, under a preheated grill (broiler) and cook for 3–5 minutes, or until softened and warm.

Fill a deep frying pan three-quarters full with cold water and add the vinegar and some salt to stop the egg whites spreading. Bring the water to a gentle simmer. Gently break an egg into a small bowl, then carefully slide the egg into the water, then repeat with the remaining eggs. Reduce the heat so that the water barely moves. Cook for 1–2 minutes, or until the eggs are just set. Remove with a spatula. Drain on paper towels.

Top each slice of toast with some spinach, an egg and some dressing. Serve with the grilled tomato halves on the side.

HINTS:
• Don't use malt vinegar in the poaching water—it contains gluten.
• Avoid cross-contamination by using separate toasters for gluten-containing and gluten-free bread. Alternatively, shake out the crumbs before each use.

THIS NUTRITIOUS MEAL IS A GREAT CHOICE FOR CHILDREN AND ADULTS WHO HAVE HAD LONG-STANDING UNTREATED COELIAC DISEASE BECAUSE IT PROVIDES SO MANY IMPORTANT NUTRIENTS, SUCH AS IRON, ZINC, FOLATE AND VITAMINS A, B12 AND D.

nutrition per serve   Energy 1772 kJ (422 Cal)

Fat 16.1 g

Saturated fat 5.4 g

Protein 26.1 g

Carbohydrate 42.5 g

Fibre 8.3 g

Cholesterol 386 mg

HOME-MADE BAKED BEANS

SOME BRANDS OF COMMERCIAL BAKED BEANS ARE NOT GLUTEN-FREE, SO STAY ON THE SAFE SIDE AND MAKE YOUR OWN. HOME-MADE BAKED BEANS ARE A GREAT CHOICE FOR PEOPLE WITH DIABETES BECAUSE THEY ARE LOW GI.

550 g (1 lb 4 oz/3 cups) dried soya beans
400 g (14 oz) tin diced tomatoes
250 ml (9 fl oz/1 cup) vegetable stock GF
   (Basics)
1 bay leaf
2 tbsp chopped parsley

pinch of dried thyme
1 tbsp canola or olive oil

PREP TIME: 5 MINUTES
COOKING TIME: 4 HOURS 40 MINUTES
SERVES 6

Cook the soya beans in plenty of water for about 4 hours, or until tender. Drain. Preheat the oven to 180°C (350°F/Gas 4).

Put the soya beans in a casserole dish and add the tinned tomatoes, stock, herbs and oil. Bake, covered, for 40 minutes. Check the consistency of the sauce. If you want a thicker consistency, remove the lid of the casserole dish and cook for a further 10–15 minutes, or until reduced to the desired consistency.

HINTS:
• Some brands of stock (ready-to-use, cubes and powder) are not gluten free, so check the ingredient list if you are using a commercial brand.
• When serving baked beans for breakfast, serve with toasted gluten-free bread. Baked beans can also be served as a light meal with rice or gluten-free corn tortillas.

nutrition per serve: Energy 1497 kJ (358 Cal); Fat 21.7 g; Saturated fat 3.1 g; Protein 29.6 g; Carbohydrate 9.9 g; Fibre 19.7 g; Cholesterol 3 mg

EGGS EN COCOTTE

YOU DON'T NECESSARILY NEED TO COOK SEPARATE MEALS FOR DIFFERENT
FAMILY MEMBERS IF ONLY ONE OF THEM NEEDS A GLUTEN-FREE DIET.
RECIPES LIKE THIS ONE CAN FEED THE WHOLE FAMILY.

1 tbsp olive oil

1 garlic clove, crushed

3 vine-ripened tomatoes (about 300 g/
    10½ oz), peeled, seeded and chopped

½ tsp olive oil, extra

4 eggs

2 tbsp snipped chives

4 slices of thick gluten-free bread

15 g (½ oz) butter

PREP TIME: 15 MINUTES

COOKING TIME: 30 MINUTES

SERVES 4

Preheat the oven to 180°C (350°F/Gas 4). To make the tomato sauce, heat the oil in a
heavy-based frying pan. Add the garlic and cook for 30 seconds. Add the tomato and
season with salt and freshly ground black pepper. Cook over medium heat for 15 minutes,
or until thickened.

Grease four 125 ml (4 fl oz/½ cup) ramekins with the extra olive oil, then carefully break
1 egg into each, trying not to break the yolk. Pour the tomato sauce evenly around the
outside of each egg, so the yolk is still visible. Sprinkle with chives and season lightly with
salt and freshly ground black pepper.

Place the ramekins in a deep baking dish and pour in enough hot water to come halfway
up the outside of the ramekins. Bake for about 10–12 minutes, or until the egg white is
set. Toast the bread and lightly spread the slices with the butter. Serve immediately with
the cooked eggs.

HINTS:
• If you are serving this to children, cut the toast into fingers to dip into the egg.
• People with coeliac disease have to be careful to avoid even small amounts of gluten,
  so make sure you use separate toasters for gluten-free and gluten-containing breads to
  avoid cross-contamination; alternatively, shake our the crumbs before each use.

nutrition per serve: Energy 1146 kJ (274 Cal); Fat 13.5 g; Saturated fat 4.4 g; Protein 10.6 g;
Carbohydrate 26.7 g; Fibre 1.6 g; Cholesterol 200 mg

HERE'S ANOTHER EGG-BASED
DISH THAT CAN BE ENJOYED
ANYTIME. THIS RECIPE SHOWS
YOU HOW EASY IT IS TO SLIP
EXTRA VEGETABLES AND
HERBS INTO YOUR DIET TO ADD
NUTRIENTS WITHOUT ADDING
TOO MANY EXTRA KILOJOULES.

nutrition per serve   Energy 1423 kJ (340 Cal)

Fat 14.2 g

Saturated fat 4.4 g

Protein 26.6 g

Carbohydrate 25.3 g

Fibre 2.3 g

Cholesterol 384 mg

HERB OMELETTE WITH TOMATOES

250 g (9 oz) red or yellow cherry tomatoes, halved
4 eggs, lightly beaten
1 handful chopped mixed herbs (e.g. parsley, chives, oregano)
2 egg whites
3 tbsp grated low-fat cheddar cheese GF
1 handful baby rocket (arugula) leaves
2 slices of gluten-free bread, toasted

PREP TIME: 15 MINUTES
COOKING TIME: 20 MINUTES
SERVES 2

Preheat the oven to 180°C (350°F/Gas 4). Line a baking tray with baking paper. Place the tomatoes, cut side up, on the prepared tray. Season well with salt and freshly ground black pepper. Bake for 15 minutes, or until softened. Reserve about one-third of the tomatoes for garnish.

Whisk together the whole eggs and mixed herbs in a bowl. Beat the egg whites in a small bowl with electric beaters until soft peaks form. Gently whisk the egg whites into the egg and herb mixture.

Preheat a grill (broiler) to medium heat. Heat a 22 cm (8½ in) omelette pan or frying pan and lightly brush with oil. Pour in half of the egg mixture and leave for 1–2 minutes, or until lightly browned underneath.

Scatter half the cheese over the egg mixture and place the pan under the grill for 1 minute, or until the egg is set and the cheese is melted. Top with half of the remaining tomatoes and half of the rocket. Fold the omelette in half and carefully slide from the pan onto a plate. Scatter half of the reserved tomatoes over the omelette.

Gently re-whisk the remaining egg mixture, then cook a second omelette in the same way as the first. Serve with the toast.

HINTS:
- If you buy ready-to-use grated cheese, check the ingredient list on the packet for any sources of gluten. In some countries, flour may be added to stop the cheese from sticking.
- Choose eggs enriched with omega-3 essential fatty acids to get more good fats in your diet. These are available in most supermarkets.
- Use baby English spinach instead of baby rocket, if you prefer.
- Even small amounts of gluten can be damaging to a person with coeliac disease. Avoid cross-contamination by using separate toasters for gluten-containing and gluten-free bread or, at the very least, shake out the crumbs between each use.

DRIED FRUIT COMPOTE

THIS FRUITY DISH CAN BE ENJOYED ON ITS OWN OR USED AS A TOPPING FOR
GLUTEN-FREE PORRIDGE, YOGHURT OR BREAKFAST CEREAL. IT'S DELICIOUS
EITHER COLD OR WARM AND IS LOADED WITH FIBRE AND ANTIOXIDANTS.

**400 g (14 oz/3 cups) dried fruit salad
mixture (dried peaches, prunes, pears,
apricots, apples and nectarines)**
500 ml (17 fl oz/2 cups) orange juice
1 tsp soft brown sugar
1–2 star anise
1 vanilla bean, halved lengthways
low-fat plain yoghurt, to serve

PREP TIME: 10 MINUTES
COOKING TIME: 15 MINUTES
SERVES 4

Put the dried fruit salad mixture in a saucepan. Add the orange juice, sugar, star anise and vanilla bean. Bring slowly to the boil, then reduce the heat, cover and leave to simmer, stirring occasionally, for 15 minutes, or until the fruit is plump and juicy.

Discard the star anise and vanilla bean. Serve the fruit drizzled with the cooking syrup. Add a dollop of yoghurt to serve.

HINTS:
• For a slightly different flavour, use a cinnamon stick and 2 cloves instead of the star anise and vanilla bean.
• If you prefer flavoured yoghurt over plain, make sure to check the label to ensure the yoghurt is free of gluten.

nutrition per serve: Energy 1239 kJ (295 Cal); Fat 0.5 g; Saturated fat 0 g; Protein 3.8 g; Carbohydrate 70.8 g; Fibre 7.9 g; Cholesterol 0 mg

FRESH FRUIT QUINOA

THIS IS A GOOD RECIPE TO TRY IF YOU'RE UNFAMILIAR WITH QUINOA, A TINY GLUTEN-FREE GRAIN. QUINOA TAKES LITTLE TIME TO PREPARE AND HAS A LIGHT TEXTURE AND MILD TASTE.

175 g (6 oz/1 cup) organic quinoa
500 ml (17 fl oz/2 cups) unsweetened
   apple and blackcurrant juice
1 cinnamon stick
2 tsp grated orange zest
2 fresh figs, chopped
2 peaches or nectarines
200 g (7 oz/1⅓ cups) strawberries, hulled
   and chopped
low-fat plain yoghurt, to serve
mint leaves, to garnish

PREP TIME: 10 MINUTES
COOKING TIME: 15 MINUTES
SERVES 4–6

Rinse the quinoa under cold running water and drain. Put the quinoa, juice and cinnamon stick in a saucepan.

Bring to the boil, cover and simmer for 10–15 minutes, or until all the liquid has been absorbed and the quinoa is translucent and the spiral germ ring is visible. Remove the cinnamon stick. Cover and set aside to firm up and cool a little.

Fold in the orange zest and half of the chopped fruit. Spoon the mixture into four bowls and sprinkle with the remaining fruit. Serve with a generous dollop of the yoghurt. Garnish with fresh mint leaves and serve immediately.

HINT:
• Quinoa is pronounced 'keen-wa'. It has been cultivated in the South American Andes for 500 years. It is now grown in and exported from Peru and the United States. Quinoa can be used as a substitute for couscous and can be found in health-food stores and in the health-food section of supermarkets.
• If you want to serve a flavoured yoghurt with this recipe, check the label to ensure the yoghurt is free of gluten.

nutrition per serve (6): Energy 737 kJ (176 Cal); Fat 1.8 g; Saturated fat 0.2 g; Protein 5.1 g; Carbohydrate 32.4 g; Fibre 3.8 g; Cholesterol 0 mg

ITALIAN-STYLE BREAKFAST TOASTS

4 Roma (plum) tomatoes, halved
2 large field mushrooms, halved
canola or olive oil spray
8 slices of low-fat bacon GF
165 g (5¾ oz/⅔ cup) plain cottage cheese
2 tbsp chopped flat-leaf (Italian) parsley
1 tbsp snipped chives
4 slices of gluten-free bread, toasted
balsamic vinegar, to drizzle

PREP TIME: 15 MINUTES
COOKING TIME: 10 MINUTES
SERVES 4

Preheat the grill (broiler). Place the tomatoes, cut side up, and the mushrooms on a large baking tray. Lightly spray with the oil. Season well with black pepper. Pat the bacon dry with paper towels and place on the tray. Grill the tomatoes, mushrooms and bacon for 5–8 minutes, or until cooked. Turn the bacon slices once and remove them as they cook and become crisp.

Combine the cottage cheese, parsley and chives. Spread thickly over the toasted bread. Arrange the tomatoes, mushrooms and bacon over the top. Drizzle with a little balsamic vinegar, then serve while hot.

HINTS:
- Gluten can be found in the most unlikely of sources, such as bacon. Check the label on the packet to ensure you buy gluten-free bacon.
- This recipe will work best with a gluten-free bread that toasts well. You may need to experiment with different types before you find the bread that toasts the best.
- Remember to keep gluten-free and regular bread separate if you live in a household where not everyone eats gluten-free foods. You will need to prepare the different types of bread on different cutting boards and with separate utensils to avoid cross-contamination. You may even need separate toasters or you will need to thoroughly shake out the crumbs from the toaster before you toast your gluten-free bread. Alternatively, some organizations helping people with coeliac disease sell protective bags to cover bread while it is being toasted. It is a great invention that makes it easier to avoid cross-contamination if you don't have separate toasters.

By using low-fat bacon in this meal, you can still enjoy a great bacon flavour without too much fat. The variety of foods (meat, vegetables, dairy and grain products) provides flavour and good amounts of many vital nutrients.

nutrition per serve   Energy 954 kJ (278 Cal)
Fat 5 g
Saturated fat 2.5 g
Protein 21.1 g
Carbohydrate 25.4 g
Fibre 1.7 g
Cholesterol 29 mg

SNACKS, LIGHT MEALS AND SIDES

PUFFED CORN SNACK MIX

360 g (12¾ oz/12 cups) gluten-free puffed
   corn breakfast cereal
400 g (14 oz) packet dried fruit and raw
   nut mixture
90 g (3¼ oz/1 cup) rice bran
55 g (2 oz/1 cup) flaked coconut, toasted
4 tbsp pepitas (pumpkin seeds)
260 g (9¼ oz/¾ cup) honey

PREP TIME: 10 MINUTES
COOKING TIME: 20 MINUTES
SERVES 20

Preheat the oven to 180°C (350°F/Gas 4). Line four baking trays with baking paper. Place the puffed corn, dried fruit and nut mixture, bran, flaked coconut and pepitas in a large bowl and mix together well.

Heat the honey in a saucepan over low heat for 3 minutes, or until it thins to a pouring consistency. Pour over the puffed corn mixture and stir until all the dry ingredients are well coated with the honey.

Spread the mixture on the lined baking trays in a single layer and bake for 15 minutes, or until golden, turning the cereal several times during cooking. Cool completely before storing in an airtight container in a cool, dark place.

HINTS:
• If you want to lower the fat content, leave out the flaked coconut.
• Pepitas are peeled pumpkin seeds—they are available at most supermarkets and health-food stores, and they make a tasty snack.

MANY COMMERCIAL SNACK FOODS CONTAIN GLUTEN, SO MAKING YOUR OWN GLUTEN-FREE SNACKS MAKES SENSE. YOU CAN EASILY PACK A SMALL CONTAINER OF THIS MIX TO TAKE WITH YOU TO WORK, SCHOOL OR WHEN TRAVELLING.

nutrition per serve   Energy 1126 kJ (269 Cal)
Fat 15.8 g
Saturated fat 2.1 g
Protein 20 g
Carbohydrate 7.9 g
Fibre 12.1 g
Cholesterol 3 mg

TAMARI NUT MIX

This yummy nut and seed mix is great for people who love savoury snacks and is perfect for when you entertain. The nuts and seeds add a lot of fat (mostly unsaturated), so enjoy in moderation.

235 g (8½ oz/1¾ cups) mixed raw unsalted
  nuts (almonds, Brazil nuts, peanuts,
  walnuts)
110 g (3¾ oz/¾ cup) pepitas (pumpkin
  seeds)
125 g (4½ oz/1 cup) sunflower seeds
115 g (4 oz/¾ cup) raw unsalted cashew
  nuts
150 g (5½ oz/scant 1 cup) raw unsalted
  macadamia nuts
125 ml (4 fl oz/½ cup) tamari GF

PREP TIME: 10 MINUTES +
  10 MINUTES STANDING
COOKING TIME: 25 MINUTES
MAKES 750 G (1 LB 10 OZ/4 CUPS)
SERVES 12

Preheat the oven to 140°C (275°F/Gas 1). You will need two large baking trays.

Place the mixed nuts, pepitas, sunflower seeds, cashew nuts and macadamia nuts in a large bowl. Pour the tamari over the nuts and seeds, then toss together well, coating them evenly. Set aside for 10 minutes.

Spread the nut and seed mixture evenly over the baking trays and bake for 20–25 minutes, or until dry-roasted as desired. Cool completely.

HINTS:
• Dry-roasted nuts may be dusted with wheat flour, so make sure you use raw gluten-free nuts in this recipe.
• Tamari is a fermented soy product similar to soy sauce. It is made with 100 per cent whole soya beans, so it is much stronger than regular soy sauce and you don't need to use as much. Tamari is traditionally free of wheat but check the label to ensure it is also free of gluten.
• Don't worry if the nut mixture does not seem crisp when you take it out of the oven. It won't crisp to its full potential until it is cooled. Store in an airtight container away from direct sunlight for up to 2 weeks. If the nut mixture becomes soft, lay the nuts on a baking tray and bake in a 150°C (300°F/Gas 2) oven for 5–10 minutes.

nutrition per serve: Energy 1611 kJ (385 Cal); Fat 34.3 g; Saturated fat 4.5 g; Protein 12.2 g; Carbohydrate 5.7 g; Fibre 5.1 g; Cholesterol 0 mg

HUMMUS

NO WONDER HUMMUS IS POPULAR! IT'S SO DELICIOUS AND VERSATILE. IT CAN BE SERVED AS A DIP WITH FRESH VEGETABLE STICKS AND GLUTEN-FREE CRACKERS OR USED AS A LOW-FAT SUBSTITUTE FOR MARGARINE OR BUTTER.

220 g (7¾ oz/1 cup) dried chickpeas
2 tbsp tahini GF
4 garlic cloves, crushed
4 tbsp lemon juice, plus extra (optional)
2 tbsp olive oil
2 tsp ground cumin
large pinch of cayenne pepper
½ tsp salt
paprika, to sprinkle
1 tbsp chopped parsley

PREP TIME: 20 MINUTES +
OVERNIGHT SOAKING
COOKING TIME: 1¼ HOURS
SERVES 20

Put the chickpeas in a large bowl, cover with plenty of water and leave to soak overnight. Drain, then rinse well.

Transfer the chickpeas to a large saucepan and cover with cold water. Bring to the boil, then reduce the heat and simmer for 1¼ hours, or until the chickpeas are very tender, occasionally skimming any froth from the surface. Drain well, reserving about 250 ml (9 fl oz/1 cup) of the cooking liquid. Leave the chickpeas until cool enough to handle. Pick over for any loose skins and discard.

Process the chickpeas, tahini, garlic, lemon juice, olive oil, cumin, salt and cayenne pepper in a food processor until thick and smooth. With the motor still running, gradually add about 185 ml (6 fl oz/¾ cup) of the reserved cooking liquid to form a smooth creamy purée. Add extra lemon juice, to taste, if necessary.

Spread onto a flat bowl or plate, sprinkle with paprika and scatter the parsley over the top.

HINTS:
• Tahini is a thick paste made of ground sesame seeds. It is available at large supermarkets and health-food shops.
• Serve with vegetable crudités or gluten-free crackers.

nutrition per serve: Energy 245 kJ (58 Cal); Fat 3.7 g; Saturated fat 0.5 g; Protein 2.2 g; Carbohydrate 3.8 g; Fibre 1.7 g; Cholesterol 0 mg

THIS LOW-FAT EGGPLANT
SAMBAL CAN BE SERVED AS A
SIDE DISH WITH CURRY AND
RICE OR ENJOYED AS A TASTY
DIP WITH GLUTEN-FREE BREAD,
CRACKERS OR POPPADOMS.

nutrition per serve

Energy 232 kJ (55 Cal)
Fat 1.9 g
Saturated fat 0.6 g
Protein 3 g
Carbohydrate 5.9 g
Fibre 3.3 g
Cholesterol 4 mg

EGGPLANT SAMBAL

2 eggplants (aubergines), halved
canola or olive oil spray
½ tsp ground turmeric
3 tbsp lime juice
2 red chillies, seeded and finely chopped
1 red onion, finely chopped
4 tbsp plain yoghurt

PREP TIME: 15 MINUTES
COOKING TIME: 30 MINUTES
SERVES 4

Preheat the oven to 200°C (400°F/Gas 6). Put the eggplants in a roasting tin, cut side up. Spray the cut halves of the eggplants with the oil and sprinkle with the turmeric. Roast for 30 minutes, or until they are browned all over and very soft.

Scoop the eggplant pulp into a bowl, then mash with the lime juice, chilli and red onion, reserving some chilli and onion for garnish.

Season with salt, then fold in the yoghurt. Garnish with the remaining onion and chilli.

HINTS:
• This is quite a chunky dip so it needs something crispy to scoop it up. Try gluten-free poppadoms or crackers.
• This dip can also be served as an accompaniment to curries or stir-fries, with some rice to provide a respite from the chilli.

WHITE BEAN AND CHICKPEA DIP

THIS LOW-GI DIP IS A DELICIOUS WAY TO EAT LEGUMES. IT CAN BE SERVED
WITH FRESH VEGETABLES AND TOASTED GLUTEN-FREE TORTILLA PIECES AS A
SNACK OR USED IN PLACE OF MARGARINE OR BUTTER.

400 g (14 oz) tin cannellini (white) beans GF,
   drained and rinsed
400 g (14 oz) tin chickpeas GF, drained and
   rinsed
1½ tsp ground cumin
3 garlic cloves, crushed
2 tbsp chopped flat-leaf (Italian) parsley
3 tbsp lemon juice
1 tsp grated lemon zest
1 tbsp tahini GF

PREP TIME: 10 MINUTES
COOKING TIME: NIL
SERVES 3–4

Place all ingredients in a food processor and process for 30 seconds. With the motor still running, slowly add 3 tablespoons hot water to the processor in a thin stream until the mixture is smooth and 'dippable'. Serve at room temperature with fresh vegetable sticks and gluten-free bread, crackers, rice cakes or toasted pieces of tortilla.

HINTS:
• Tahini is a thick paste made of ground sesame seeds. It is available at large supermarkets and health-food shops.
• Remember to read the ingredient list on the tins of cannellini beans and chickpeas to ensure that they are free of gluten; plain tinned legumes usually are, but it's important to check in case a manufacturer uses a gluten-containing additive or preservative.

nutrition per serve (4): Energy 701 kJ (167 Cal); Fat 4.7 g; Saturated fat 0.6 g; Protein 10.2 g; Carbohydrate 17.7 g; Fibre 8.3 g; Cholesterol 0 mg

MUSHROOM PÂTÉ

COMMERCIALLY MADE PÂTÉS CAN CONTAIN GLUTEN BUT YOU DON'T HAVE TO
MISS OUT IF YOU MAKE YOUR OWN. THIS ONE IS SUITABLE FOR VEGETARIANS
AND LOWER IN FAT THAN MANY COMMERCIAL VARIETIES.

1 tsp olive oil
1 small onion, chopped
2 garlic cloves, crushed
300 g (10½ oz) flat mushrooms, wiped
  clean and chopped
4 tbsp dry white wine or water
80 g (2¾ oz/1 cup) fresh gluten-free
  breadcrumbs
2 tbsp thyme, plus extra to serve
2 tbsp chopped flat-leaf (Italian) parsley
1 tbsp lemon juice

PREP TIME: 15 MINUTES +
  1 HOUR REFRIGERATION
COOKING TIME: 10 MINUTES
SERVES 4–6

Heat the oil in a large, deep frying pan. Add the onion and garlic and cook, stirring, for
2 minutes without browning. Add the mushrooms and white wine or water. Cook, stirring
for 1 minute, then cover and simmer for 5 minutes, stirring once or twice. Remove the lid
and increase the heat to evaporate any liquid. Cool.

Place the mushroom mixture, breadcrumbs, herbs and lemon juice in a food processor.
Process until smooth and season well with salt and black pepper. Spoon into a serving
bowl. Cover and refrigerate for at least 1 hour to allow the flavours to develop.

HINTS:
• You'll need about 3 average slices of gluten-free bread without crusts for the amount of
  breadcrumbs you need for the pâté. To make the breadcrumbs, blend the bread in a food
  processor until crumbs form.
• Serve with gluten-free bread or crackers.

nutrition per serve (6): Energy 320 kJ (76 Cal); Fat 1.1 g; Saturated fat 0.2 g; Protein 3.3 g;
Carbohydrate 10.1 g; Fibre 2.2 g; Cholesterol 1 mg

MINI POTATO AND LEEK QUICHES

**600 g (1 lb 5 oz) boiling potatoes, peeled
and chopped**
2 tbsp canola or olive oil
**300 g (10½ oz/2 cups) gluten-free
self-raising flour**
1 tsp gluten-free baking powder
1 tsp salt
2 eggs

FILLING
40 g (1½ oz) butter
1 leek, washed and thinly sliced
3 eggs
185 ml (6 fl oz/¾ cup) milk
185 g (6½ oz/¾ cup) sour cream

PREP TIME: 20 MINUTES
COOKING TIME: 50 MINUTES
MAKES 24

Preheat the oven to 180°C (350°F/Gas 4). Lightly grease two 12-hole round-based patty pans. Boil or steam the potatoes for 15 minutes, or until tender. Drain well, then mash until smooth. You will need 450 g (1 lb/2 cups) warm mashed potato for this recipe.

Combine the mashed potato and oil in a large bowl. Sift in the flour and baking powder, then add the salt and enough egg to mix to a smooth dough. Lightly dust a board with gluten-free flour, then knead the dough on this board until smooth. Roll out the pastry until it is 5 mm (¼ in) thick. Cut into 6–7 cm (2½–2¾ in) rounds and place in the prepared pans. Bake for 5 minutes, then remove from the oven and press out any air bubbles in the pastry. Cool completely. Increase the oven temperature to 200°C (400°F/Gas 6).

To make the filling, melt the butter in a heavy-based saucepan over medium heat. Add the leek and cook, stirring often, for 5–6 minutes until tender. Set aside to cool. Season with salt and freshly ground black pepper.

Whisk the eggs, milk and sour cream together in a bowl until well combined. Divide the leek mixture evenly among the pastry cases, then pour the egg mixture over the filling. Bake for 15–20 minutes, or until set and golden brown. Serve hot or cold.

HINTS:
• The quiches can be made the day before and refrigerated in an airtight container. Reheat for 10 minutes in a 150°C (300°F/Gas 2) oven.
• These mini vegetarian quiches can be enjoyed as a light meal or served as finger food at a party. Enjoy in moderation because they are high in fat. You can use low-fat milk and light sour cream to lower the fat content if you are concerned about the fat content.

AFTER STARTING A GLUTEN-FREE
DIET YOU MAY HAVE THOUGHT
YOU'D NEVER BE ABLE TO ENJOY
QUICHE AGAIN, BUT IT'S EASY TO
MAKE A GLUTEN-FREE VERSION.

nutrition per quiche

Energy 579 kJ (138 Cal)

Fat 7.7 g

Saturated fat 3.7 g

Protein 3 g

Carbohydrate 13.7 g

Fibre 1.5 g

Cholesterol 55 mg

MINI SWEET POTATO QUICHES

THESE MINI QUICHES CAN BE SERVED AS A SNACK OR FINGER FOOD, BUT DON'T GO OVERBOARD BECAUSE THEY'RE NOT LOW IN KILOJOULES. YOU CAN USE LOW-FAT MILK AND LIGHT SOUR CREAM TO LOWER THE FAT CONTENT.

450 g (1 lb/3 cups) gluten-free plain (all-purpose) flour
200 g (7 oz) butter
2 eggs, lightly beaten

SWEET POTATO FILLING
400 g (14 oz) sweet potato, peeled and cut into 1 cm (½ in) dice
canola or olive oil spray

200 g (7 oz) ricotta cheese, crumbled
2 tbsp snipped chives
3 eggs
185 ml (6 fl oz/¾ cup) milk
185 g (6½ oz/¾ cup) sour cream

PREP TIME: 25 MINUTES
COOKING TIME: 35 MINUTES
MAKES 24

Preheat the oven to 200°C (400°F/Gas 6). Lightly grease a baking tray and two 12-hole round-based patty pans.

Sift the flour into a large bowl. Rub in the butter with your fingertips until the mixture resembles dry breadcrumbs. Make a well in the centre and add the lightly beaten eggs and 1–2 tablespoons water, or enough to form a soft dough. Lightly dust a board with gluten-free flour, then put the dough on the board and knead lightly. Lightly dust two large sheets of baking paper with gluten-free flour, then roll out the pastry between these sheets to about 3 mm (⅛ in) thick. Cut the dough into 6–7 cm (2½–2¾ in) rounds and place in the prepared patty pans. The dough should make 24 rounds.

To make the sweet potato filling, put the sweet potato on the prepared tray. Spray with oil and season with a little salt and pepper. Bake for 15 minutes, or until golden brown. Cool. Combine the sweet potato with the crumbled ricotta cheese and snipped chives.

Combine the eggs, milk and sour cream in a bowl until well combined. Divide the sweet potato mixture evenly among the pastry cases, then pour the egg mixture over the filling. Bake for 15–20 minutes, or until golden brown. Serve hot or cold.

HINT:
• The quiches can be made the day before and refrigerated in an airtight container. Reheat for 10 minutes in a 150°C (300°F/Gas 2) oven.

nutrition per quiche: Energy 858 kJ (205 Cal); Fat 12.7 g; Saturated fat 7.7 g; Protein 3.2 g; Carbohydrate 19.3 g; Fibre 0.6 g; Cholesterol 76 mg

CRISPY WAFER BISCUITS

THESE LIGHT CRISPY BISCUITS ARE GOOD ON THEIR OWN OR SERVED WITH ONE OF THE DIPS ON THE PREVIOUS PAGES. IF YOU HAVE KIDS WHO NEED GLUTEN-FREE SNACKS YOU'LL BE ASKED TO MAKE THESE REGULARLY.

175 g (6 oz/1 cup) rice flour
125 g (4½ oz/1 cup) pure maize cornflour
(cornstarch) GF
40 g (1½ oz/½ cup) rice bran
½ tsp salt
2 tbsp canola or olive oil

PREP TIME: 10 MINUTES
COOKING TIME: 25 MINUTES
MAKES ABOUT 40

Preheat the oven to 200°C (400°F/Gas 6). Lightly grease two 30 x 25 cm (12 x 10 in) Swiss roll (jelly roll) tins.

Combine the dry ingredients in a bowl and make a well in the middle. In a separate bowl mix together 185 ml (6 fl oz/¾ cup) water and the oil, then pour into the well in the dry ingredients. Mix until thoroughly combined.

Divide the mixture into two portions. Press each portion of dough into one of the prepared tins and bake for 20–25 minutes. Cool in the tin. Break into pieces and store in an airtight container for up to 2 days.

HINT:
• If you'd like more evenly shaped biscuits, score the dough in the tins with a knife before you bake them, then the biscuits will be easy to break neatly once they're cooked.

nutrition per serve: Energy 173 kJ (41 Cal); Fat 1.3 g; Saturated fat 0.2 g; Protein 0.4 g; Carbohydrate 6.6 g; Fibre 0.4 g; Cholesterol 0 mg

THESE WILL BE HARD TO RESIST WHETHER YOU NEED A GLUTEN-FREE DIET OR NOT. TAKE A PLATE OF THESE WITH YOU WHEN YOU'RE INVITED TO A FRIEND'S HOUSE, SO THERE'S SOMETHING SUITABLE FOR YOU TO EAT—BUT BE PREPARED TO FIGHT FOR THEM.

nutrition per serve

Energy 325 kJ (78 Cal)
Fat 5.3 g
Saturated fat 1.5 g
Protein 2.6 g
Carbohydrate 5 g
Fibre 0.2 g
Cholesterol 32 mg

CHICKEN AND LEEK PUFFS

4 tbsp canola or olive oil

115 g (4 oz/¾ cup) gluten-free plain (all-purpose) flour

¼ tsp bicarbonate of soda (baking soda)

¾ tsp gluten-free baking powder

3 eggs

CHICKEN AND LEEK FILLING

40 g (1½ oz) butter

150 g (5½ oz) boneless, skinless chicken breast

½ leek, washed and thinly sliced

1 tbsp gluten-free plain (all-purpose) flour

3 tbsp milk

3 tbsp chicken stock GF (Basics)

1 tbsp chopped parsley

PREP TIME: 1 HOUR

COOKING TIME: 40 MINUTES

MAKES 24

Preheat the oven to 210°C (415°F/Gas 6–7). Cover two baking trays with baking paper. Pour 250 ml (9 fl oz/1 cup) water and the oil into a saucepan and bring to the boil. Remove from the heat, add the sifted dry ingredients, then return to the heat and stir constantly until the mixture thickens and leaves the side of the saucepan (it may look a little oily). Scoop into the small bowl of an electric mixer and set aside to cool slightly.

Beat the mixture, adding the eggs one at a time and beating well between each addition, until it is thick and shiny. Place level tablespoons of the mixture onto the prepared trays. Spray lightly all over with cold water, to aid rising. Bake for 10 minutes, or until they rise and start to brown. Reduce the heat to 190°C (375°F/Gas 5) and bake for 10–15 minutes, or until cooked through. Remove the puffs from the oven and leave to cool on a wire rack.

To make the chicken and leek filling, melt 1 tablespoon of the butter in a frying pan over medium heat, add the chicken breast and fry for 3 minutes on each side, or until cooked through. Remove from the pan and cut into small pieces. Melt the remaining butter in a saucepan, add the leek and cook, stirring often, for 5–6 minutes, or until soft. Sprinkle the flour over the leek and cook, stirring, for 20 seconds. Add the combined milk and stock, stirring over the heat until the mixture boils and thickens. Season with a little salt and pepper. Add the chicken and parsley to the sauce and heat gently until warmed through.

Split the puffs in half, spoon in the warm filling, then replace the tops. Serve while warm.

HINT:
• The puffs can be made and stored unfilled in an airtight container for 1 week. If they become soft, reheat them in a 150°C (300°F/Gas 2) oven for 5–10 minutes.

GLAZED DRUMSTICKS

THESE DRUMSTICKS WILL SUIT PEOPLE WHO ALSO HAVE OTHER FOOD
INTOLERANCES BECAUSE THEY ARE FREE OF WHEAT, GLUTEN, NUT, EGG AND
DAIRY. THEY ARE A GOOD ADDITION TO A LUNCH BOX OR PICNIC HAMPER.

8 large chicken drumsticks (skin removed)
4 tbsp golden syrup or honey
3 tbsp pear juice
1 tbsp canola or olive oil
1 tsp salt

PREP TIME: 20 MINUTES +
OVERNIGHT MARINATING
COOKING TIME: 40 MINUTES
SERVES 4

Put the drumsticks in a shallow non-metallic dish. Combine the remaining ingredients
and pour the marinade over the drumsticks, making sure they are all coated. Marinate
overnight, turning occasionally.

Preheat the oven to 180°C (350°F/Gas 4). Put the drumsticks and marinade into a baking
dish. Bake for 35–40 minutes, turning frequently during cooking and brushing with the pan
juices. If the pan juices start to overbrown, add a small amount of water or stock until
syrupy. Serve hot or cold.

HINT:
• Serve these as a snack or with a selection of salads for a meal.

nutrition per serve: Energy 2311 kJ (552 Cal); Fat 23.5 g; Saturated fat 5.8 g; Protein 62.4 g;
Carbohydrate 23.8 g; Fibre 0 g; Cholesterol 267 mg

VEAL AND CHICKEN TERRINE

COMMERCIAL TERRINES AND PÂTÉS MAY CONTAIN GLUTEN. MAKE YOUR OWN
TO ENSURE YOU'RE GETTING A GLUTEN-FREE VERSION.

2 tbsp canola or olive oil

2 garlic cloves, crushed

1 leek, washed and finely chopped

1 kg (2 lb 4 oz) minced (ground) veal

1 handful snipped chives

3 eggs, lightly beaten

2 tbsp canola or olive oil, extra

3 tbsp gin

1½ tsp salt

40 g (1½ oz/½ cup) fresh gluten-free
   breadcrumbs

2 boneless, skinless chicken breasts, each
   cut into four long strips

PREP TIME: 45 MINUTES

COOKING TIME: 1½ HOURS

SERVES 6–8

Preheat the oven to 180°C (350°F/Gas 4). Grease a 20 x 10 cm (8 x 4 in) loaf (bar) tin,
then line with foil.

Heat the oil in a frying pan over medium heat, add the garlic and leek and fry for about
5 minutes, or until soft. Allow to cool. Transfer to a bowl, then add the veal, chives, eggs,
extra oil, gin, salt and breadcrumbs. Using your hands, mix and knead the mixture until it
is well combined.

Put half of the mince mixture into the prepared tin, pressing down well. Lay the chicken
breast strips over the meat. Press the remaining mince mixture over the chicken. Cover
with greased foil. Place in a baking dish and add enough boiling water to come halfway
up the sides of the loaf tin. Bake for 1¼–1½ hours.

When cooked, remove the loaf tin from the dish of water and drain off any liquid. Put a
piece of cardboard on top of the terrine, then weigh it down with a heavy weight (for
instance, tins of food). Refrigerate until cold.

HINTS:
• Make your own breadcrumbs by blending gluten-free bread in a food processor until
  crumbs form—you'll need about 1½ pieces of gluten-free bread without crusts to make
  enough for this recipe.
• Cut into thin slices and serve with salad or use as a sandwich filling.

nutrition per serve (8): Energy 1600 kJ (382 Cal); Fat 20.6 g; Saturated fat 5.2 g; Protein 41.1 g;
Carbohydrate 4.3 g; Fibre 0.5 g; Cholesterol 205 mg

ROAST PUMPKIN AND FETA PIZZA

450 g (1 lb/3 cups) gluten-free plain
(all-purpose) flour
4 tsp dried yeast GF
1/2 tsp sugar
1 tsp salt
1 1/2 tbsp canola or olive oil

TOPPING
500 g (1 lb 2 oz) pumpkin (winter squash),
peeled, seeded and chopped
canola or olive oil spray
1 tbsp canola or olive oil
2 onions, thinly sliced

2 garlic cloves, crushed
3 tbsp pine nuts
3 tbsp tomato paste (concentrated purée) GF
1 garlic clove, extra, crushed
1 tsp dried oregano
125 g (4 1/2 oz) reduced-fat feta cheese,
crumbled
4 tbsp black olives, pitted and crushed
2 tbsp thyme

PREP TIME: 45 MINUTES + 1 HOUR RISING
COOKING TIME: 1 HOUR 5 MINUTES
SERVES 4

Combine the yeast, sugar and 3 tablespoons warm water in a small bowl and set aside until foaming. Sift the flour and salt into a large bowl. In a separate bowl mix together 250 ml (9 fl oz/1 cup) warm water and the oil, then pour into the well in the dry ingredients along with the yeast mixture. Use a wooden spoon to mix until almost combined. Use your hands to mix into a soft dough.

Lightly dust a board with gluten-free flour. Turn the dough out onto the board and knead until smooth. Place the dough in a lightly oiled bowl. Cover and set aside in a warm place for 1 hour, or until the dough has doubled in size.

Meanwhile, make the topping. Preheat the oven to 180°C (350°F/Gas 4). Line a baking tray with baking paper. Put the pumpkin on the lined tray and spray with oil. Bake for 45 minutes. Set aside. Increase the oven temperature to 220°C (425°F/Gas 7). While the pumpkin is cooking, heat the oil in a large non-stick frying pan over medium heat. Add the onion and garlic and cook, stirring often, for 5 minutes, or until the onion is very soft. Stir in the pine nuts, remove from the heat and set aside. In a small bowl combine the tomato paste, garlic and oregano with 1 tablespoon water.

Use your fist to punch the dough down, then knead until it returns to its original size. Lightly grease two 27 cm (10 3/4 in) pizza trays. Divide the dough into two portions. On a surface lightly dusted with gluten-free flour, roll out one portion to fit the tray, then carefully place the dough onto the tray. Repeat with the remaining dough. Spread the tomato paste mixture evenly over each pizza base, then spread the onion mixture over this. Scatter the pumpkin, feta, olives and thyme over the top. Bake for 20 minutes, swapping the trays around once, or until the dough is golden.

HERE'S A RECIPE FOR A GLUTEN-FREE GOURMET PIZZA THAT IS A GREAT SOURCE OF THE ANTIOXIDANT BETACAROTENE, THANKS TO THE PUMPKIN. EXPERIMENT WITH DIFFERENT FLOURS TO FIND THE BEST ONE.

nutrition per serve Energy 3412 kJ (815 Cal);
Fat 30.3 g;
Saturated fat 7.6 g;
Protein 13.9 g;
Carbohydrate 117.2 g;
Fibre 6.4 g;
Cholesterol 22 mg

RICE AND COTTAGE CHEESE PIE

RICE IS AN IMPORTANT FOOD FOR PEOPLE ON GLUTEN-FREE DIETS AND CAN BE PREPARED IN MANY DIFFERENT WAYS. IN THIS RECIPE, RICE FORMS THE BASE OF A DELICIOUS PIE THAT CAN BE EATEN WARM OR COLD.

100 g (3½ oz/½ cup) white long-grain rice
2 tbsp snipped chives
30 g (1 oz) butter, melted
4 tbsp cottage cheese
2 eggs, lightly beaten

FILLING
60 g (2¼ oz) butter
5 spring onions (scallions), sliced
4 eggs
250 g (9 oz/1 cup) cottage cheese

PREP TIME: 40 MINUTES + COOLING
COOKING TIME: 1 HOUR
SERVES 4–6

Preheat the oven to 170°C (325°F/Gas 3). Lightly grease a 23 cm (9 in) flan tin or pie plate.

Bring a large saucepan of water to the boil. Add the rice and cook for 12 minutes, or until very tender, stirring occasionally. Drain and cool. You will need 280 g (10 oz/1½ cups) of cold cooked rice for this recipe. Combine the cooled rice with the chives, butter, cottage cheese and eggs and press into the base and sides of the prepared tin. Chill for 30 minutes.

Meanwhile, prepare the filling. Melt the butter in a small saucepan over low heat. Add the spring onion and cook for 8–10 minutes, or until soft, but not brown. Remove from the heat. Allow to cool.

Combine the eggs, cottage cheese and a pinch of salt in a bowl. Add the spring onion mixture and mix well. Pour the filling into the prepared crust. Bake for 40–45 minutes, or until firm and golden brown. Serve hot or cold.

HINTS:
• The rice should be very well cooked and slightly mushy. This can be achieved by stirring it once or twice during cooking.
• If you have diabetes, use a lower GI rice, such as basmati, koshikari or doongara.
• Serve the pie with a salad or on its own.

nutrition per serve (6): Energy 1285 kJ (307 Cal); Fat 20.4 g; Saturated fat 11.6 g; Protein 15.7 g; Carbohydrate 15 g; Fibre 0.5 g; Cholesterol 240 mg

SPICY LENTIL SALAD

LENTILS, LIKE ALL LEGUMES, ARE A NATURAL SUPER FOOD—THEY'RE LOW GI, A GREAT SOURCE OF FIBRE, AND PROVIDE GOOD AMOUNTS OF VITAMINS, MINERALS AND ANTIOXIDANTS.

225 g (8 oz/1 cup heaped) basmati rice
185 g (6½ oz/1 cup) brown lentils
1 tsp ground turmeric
1 tsp ground cinnamon
6 cardamom pods
3 star anise
2 bay leaves
3 tbsp canola or olive oil
1 tbsp lemon juice
250 g (9 oz) broccoli florets
2 carrots, peeled and cut into julienne
    strips
1 onion, finely chopped
2 garlic cloves, crushed
1 red capsicum (pepper), finely chopped

1 tsp garam masala
1 tsp ground coriander
250 g (9 oz/1⅔ cups) fresh or frozen peas,
    thawed if frozen

DRESSING
250 g (9 oz/1 cup) plain yoghurt
1 tbsp lemon juice
1 tbsp chopped mint
1 tsp cumin seeds

PREP TIME: 30 MINUTES
COOKING TIME: 1¼ HOURS
SERVES 6

Put the rice, lentils, turmeric, cinnamon, cardamom pods, star anise and bay leaves in a saucepan with 750 ml (26 fl oz/3 cups) water. Stir well and bring to the boil. Reduce the heat, cover and simmer gently for 50–60 minutes, or until the liquid is absorbed. Remove the whole spices. Transfer the mixture to a large bowl. Whisk 2 tablespoons of the oil with the lemon juice, then fork through the rice mixture.

Steam or boil the broccoli and carrots until tender. Drain and refresh in cold water.

Heat the remaining oil in a large frying pan and add the onion, garlic and capsicum. Stir-fry for 2–3 minutes, then add the garam masala and coriander and stir-fry for a further 1–2 minutes. Add the cooked vegetables and peas and toss to coat in the spice mixture. Add to the rice and fork through to combine. Cover and refrigerate until cold.

To make the dressing, mix the yoghurt, lemon juice, mint and cumin seeds together, then season with salt and freshly ground black pepper. Spoon the salad into six individual bowls or onto a platter and top with the dressing.

nutrition per serve: Energy 1601 kJ (381 Cal); Fat 12 g; Saturated fat 1.4 g; Protein 17.4 g; Carbohydrate 51.5 g; Fibre 11.2 g; Cholesterol 4 mg

IF YOU'RE NEW TO GLUTEN-FREE COOKING AND STILL WONDERING HOW YOU CAN USE INGREDIENTS LIKE BUCKWHEAT, TRY THIS RECIPE. IT'S A GLUTEN-FREE VERSION OF TABOULEH. IT'S VERY VERSATILE AND CAN BE EATEN AS A SNACK, SANDWICH FILLING OR SIDE SALAD.

nutrition per serve (6)   Energy 751 kJ (179 Cal)
Fat 7.1 g
Saturated fat 1 g
Protein 5.2 g
Carbohydrate 20.9 g
Fibre 5.8 g
Cholesterol 0 mg

ROASTED BUCKWHEAT TABOULEH

165 g (5¾ oz/1 cup) roasted buckwheat
   kernels (groats)
300 g (10½ oz/2 large bunches) flat-leaf
   (Italian) parsley
1 handful mint
4 spring onions (scallions), thinly sliced
4 tomatoes, finely chopped
2 garlic cloves, crushed

3 tbsp lemon juice
2 tbsp olive oil

PREP TIME: 30 MINUTES +
   15 MINUTES SOAKING
COOKING TIME: NIL
SERVES 4–6

Put the buckwheat in a bowl. Pour in enough water to cover the buckwheat and leave to soak for 15 minutes, or until the buckwheat has softened a little. Drain well, then spread onto a clean tea towel (dish towel) to dry.

Finely chop the parsley and mint with a large knife or in a food processor. If you are using a food processor, take care not to over-process.

Put the buckwheat, herbs, spring onion and tomato in a large bowl. To make the dressing, combine the garlic, lemon juice and oil in a jar with a tight-fitting lid and shake well. Pour the dressing over the salad and toss well. Refrigerate until required. Return to room temperature to serve.

HINTS:
• Buckwheat kernels are the inner shell of the husked buckwheat grain—the outer husk is inedible. Roasted buckwheat kernels look like little stones and can be bought from health-food stores. Raw buckwheat kernels can taste slightly bitter so if you buy unroasted buckwheat kernels, dry-roast them for a few minutes. It may take you a little while to get used to the crunch of the buckwheat.
• If you like, you can boost the flavour of the salad by using 3 garlic cloves, doubling the amount of lemon juice and adding an extra tablespoon of olive oil.

CANNELLINI BEAN AND ROCKET SALAD

THIS COLOURFUL SALAD CAN BE SERVED AS A SIDE DISH, SNACK OR LIGHT VEGETARIAN MEAL.

3 red capsicums (peppers), halved and
   seeded
1 garlic clove, crushed
grated zest of 1 lemon
2 handfuls coarsely chopped flat-leaf
   (Italian) parsley
400 g (14 oz) tin cannellini (white) beans GF,
   drained and rinsed
2 tbsp lemon juice

2 tbsp extra-virgin olive oil
100 g (3½ oz/1 small bunch) rocket
   (arugula) or mixed salad leaves

PREP TIME: 20 MINUTES
COOKING TIME: 15 MINUTES
SERVES 2 AS A MAIN COURSE OR
   4 AS A STARTER

Preheat a grill (broiler) to medium. Roast the capsicum, skin side up, until the skin blackens and blisters. Set aside in a plastic bag for 5 minutes, then peel away the skin and slice the flesh into strips.

Combine the garlic, lemon zest and parsley in a bowl.

Put the cannellini beans in a bowl and add half of the parsley mixture, 1 tablespoon lemon juice, 1 tablespoon extra-virgin olive oil and salt and pepper to taste. Toss together. Place the rocket or salad leaves on a large plate and dress with the remaining lemon juice and extra-virgin olive oil.

Scatter the bean mixture over the leaves, then lay the capsicum strips on top, along with the remaining parsley mixture. Season with salt and pepper and serve immediately.

HINTS:
• When using tinned beans, check the label to ensure that the manufacturer has not used any additives that contain gluten.
• Instead of tinned beans, you can soak 250 g (9 oz/1¼ cups) dried beans overnight, then boil with a dash of oil and no salt for 30–40 minutes, or until tender.
• The capsicums, herbs and lemon juice add vitamin C, which can help the amount of iron you absorb from the beans.

nutrition per serve (4): Energy 728 kJ (174 Cal); Fat 9.7 g; Saturated fat 1.3 g; Protein 7.1 g; Carbohydrate 12.4 g; Fibre 5.9 g; Cholesterol 0 mg

ROAST MUSHROOM AND BABY BEAN SALAD

THIS SALAD IS A GOOD SOURCE OF B-GROUP VITAMINS, MAKING IT A WISE CHOICE FOR PEOPLE RECOVERING FROM LONG-STANDING COELIAC DISEASE.

600 g (1 lb 5 oz) field mushrooms, brushed clean

2 tbsp olive oil

3 garlic cloves, crushed

2 tbsp lemon juice

6 French shallots, root ends trimmed, skin left on

1½ tbsp tarragon vinegar

2 tsp finely chopped tarragon

1 tbsp finely chopped flat-leaf (Italian) parsley

200 g (7 oz) baby green beans, trimmed

2 handfuls rocket (arugula)

PREP TIME: 15 MINUTES

COOKING TIME: 35 MINUTES

SERVES 4

Preheat the oven to 200°C (400°F/Gas 6). Place the mushrooms in a single layer in a large roasting tin. Add the oil, garlic, lemon juice and shallots and gently toss until coated. Roast for 30 minutes, occasionally spooning over the juices. Remove from the oven and cool to room temperature. Slip the shallots from their skins and discard the skin.

Pour the cooking juices into a large mixing bowl. Add the tarragon vinegar, tarragon and parsley. Mix and season well.

Blanch the beans in boiling salted water for 2 minutes, or until just tender. Drain well and, while still hot, add to the dressing. Set aside to cool to room temperature.

Cut the mushrooms into quarters, or eighths if large, and add to the beans along with the shallots and rocket. Gently toss together and serve on a platter or four individual plates.

HINT:
• Tarragon vinegar is available at most supermarkets or delicatessens. Alternatively, use white wine vinegar if tarragon vinegar is not available. Do not use malt vinegar because it contains gluten.

nutrition per serve: Energy 638 kJ (151 Cal); Fat 9.9 g; Saturated fat 1.3 g; Protein 7.3 g; Carbohydrate 4.8 g; Fibre 6.2 g; Cholesterol 0 mg

POTATO AND PUMPKIN SOUP

1 tbsp canola or olive oil
1 leek, halved lengthways, washed and
    sliced
2 garlic cloves, crushed
500 g (1 lb 2 oz) all-purpose potatoes,
    peeled and chopped
500 g (1 lb 2 oz) butternut pumpkin
    (squash), peeled, seeded and chopped

1.25 litres (44 fl oz/5 cups) vegetable
    stock GF (Basics)
snipped chives, to serve
gluten-free bread, to serve

PREP TIME: 30 MINUTES
COOKING TIME: 40 MINUTES
SERVES 4

Heat the oil in a large saucepan over medium heat. Add the leek and garlic and cook, stirring, for 2 minutes. Reduce the heat to low. Cover the pan with a lid and cook, stirring occasionally, for 7–8 minutes, or until the leek is very soft.

Add the potato, pumpkin and stock to the pan. Bring to the boil. Reduce the heat and simmer, partially covered, for 20–25 minutes, or until the vegetables are very soft. Set the pan aside for 10 minutes to allow the mixture to cool slightly.

Purée the soup in a blender or food processor (in batches, if necessary) until smooth. Divide the soup among four bowls and sprinkle with chives. Serve with gluten-free bread.

HINTS:
• If you're using a commercial stock, check the label to ensure it has no ingredients that contain gluten. Even better, make your own—it is much healthier and you can ensure that it contains no gluten.
• If you can tolerate dairy foods, add 2 teaspoons of light sour cream or plain yoghurt to each bowl of soup before serving.
• Diabetics should limit their intake of this soup because it has a relatively high-GI value (due to the potatoes and pumpkin) so will cause a high blood-sugar response.

THIS VIBRANT SOUP CAN BE
SERVED AS A STARTER, SNACK OR
MEAL (ADD SOME GLUTEN-FREE
BREAD). IT MAY BE PARTICULARLY
APPEALING TO FUSSY EATERS AS
IT'S A RELATIVELY SIMPLE SOUP.

nutrition per serve   Energy 837 kJ (200 Cal)
Fat 6.2 g
Saturated fat 1.1 g
Protein 6.2 g
Carbohydrate 27.7 g
Fibre 7 g
Cholesterol 25 mg

FISH AND BEAN SOUP

MANY PEOPLE DON'T EAT THE THREE OR MORE SERVES OF FISH EACH WEEK
THAT IS RECOMMENDED BY NUTRITIONISTS. THIS SOUP IS A DELICIOUS AND
SIMPLE WAY FOR YOU TO INCLUDE FISH IN YOUR DIET.

2 tbsp canola or olive oil
1 large leek, washed and thinly sliced
500 g (1 lb 2 oz) boiling potatoes, peeled
   and chopped
2 garlic cloves, crushed
1.5 litres (52 fl oz/6 cups) chicken stock GF
   (Basics)
250 g (9 oz) green beans, cut into 3 cm
   (1¼ in) pieces

500 g (1 lb 2 oz) firm white boneless fish,
   cut into small cubes
3 spring onions (scallions), thinly sliced on
   the diagonal

PREP TIME: 15 MINUTES
COOKING TIME: 30 MINUTES
SERVES 4

Heat the oil in a large saucepan over medium heat. Cook the leek, stirring often, for 5–6 minutes, or until it softens.

Add the potato and garlic and cook, stirring, for 2 minutes. Pour in the stock, increase the heat to high and bring to the boil. Reduce the heat and simmer, partially covered, for 10 minutes, or until the potato is almost tender when tested with the point of a knife.

Add the beans and fish and continue to cook for a further 5 minutes, or until the fish and beans are cooked. Stir in the spring onions. Season to taste with salt and pepper.

HINTS:
• Many commercial stocks contain gluten. If you are not using home-made stock, check the ingredient list carefully.
• If you have diabetes, you can replace the high-GI potatoes with a lower GI alternative, such as tinned chickpeas or cannellini (white) beans; this will ensure your blood-sugar response is not as high.

nutrition per serve: Energy 1487 kJ (355 Cal); Fat 12.7 g; Saturated fat 2 g; Protein 36 g; Carbohydrate 21.8 g; Fibre 4.8 g; Cholesterol 81 mg

RED LENTIL AND PARSNIP SOUP

THIS HEARTY SOUP IS A GREAT WAY TO EAT SEVERAL DIFFERENT VEGETABLES
IN ONE MEAL. IF YOU HAVE DIABETES, YOU CAN LOWER THE SOUP'S GI BY
SWAPPING THE PARSNIP WITH A SMALL SWEET POTATO.

1 tsp olive oil
1 onion, chopped
2 garlic cloves, crushed
1 parsnip, peeled and chopped
1 celery stalk, chopped
1 large carrot, peeled and chopped
1 tsp ground cumin
1 tbsp tomato paste (concentrated
    purée) GF
400 g (14 oz) tin diced tomatoes

185 g (6½ oz/¾ cup) red lentils
1 litre (35 fl oz/4 cups) chicken or
    vegetable stock GF (Basics) or water
1 tbsp lemon juice
1 handful chopped flat-leaf (Italian) parsley
gluten-free bread, to serve

PREP TIME: 20 MINUTES
COOKING TIME: 30 MINUTES
SERVES 4

Heat the oil in a large, heavy-based saucepan. Add the onion and garlic and stir-fry for
2 minutes, or until softened. Add the parsnip, celery and carrot and cook, covered, over low
heat for 8 minutes to sweat the vegetables. Stir once or twice, taking care not to brown.

Stir in the cumin, tomato paste, tomatoes, lentils and stock or water. Bring to the boil,
then reduce the heat and simmer for 20 minutes, or until the lentils are cooked. Season
well with salt and pepper. Stir in the lemon juice and parsley. Serve with gluten-free bread.

HINTS:
• If you're using a commercial brand of stock check the label to ensure it is free of gluten.
• This is a thick soup; if you prefer, add more stock or water to make it thinner.
• You can freeze the soup in serving-sized portions for up to 1 month.

nutrition per serve: Energy 972 kJ (232 Cal); Fat 2.8 g; Saturated fat 0.4 g; Protein 17.3 g;
Carbohydrate 30.5 g; Fibre 10 g; Cholesterol 5 mg

TAKE YOUR TASTE BUDS ON AN
EXOTIC JOURNEY WITH THIS CLASSIC
ASIAN SOUP. IT'S A COMPLETE LOW-
GI MEAL IN A BOWL THAT PROVIDES
GOOD AMOUNTS OF IRON, ZINC,
VITAMIN B12 AND FOLATE. THE
FRAGRANT HERBS AND SPICES WILL
AWAKEN YOUR SENSES.

nutrition per serve

Energy 1367 kJ (326 Cal)
Fat 6.1 g
Saturated fat 2.4 g
Protein 31.2 g
Carbohydrate 35.9 g
Fibre 2.5 g
Cholesterol 64 mg

VIETNAMESE BEEF SOUP

400 g (14 oz) lean rump steak, trimmed
½ onion
1½ tbsp fish sauce GF
1 star anise
1 cinnamon stick
pinch of ground white pepper
1.5 litres (52 fl oz/6 cups) beef stock GF
  (Basics)
300 g (10½ oz) thin fresh rice noodles
3 spring onions (scallions), thinly sliced
1 small handful Vietnamese mint

90 g (3¼ oz/1 cup) bean sprouts, trimmed
1 small onion, halved and thinly sliced
1 small red chilli, thinly sliced on the
  diagonal
lemon wedges, to serve

PREP TIME: 20 MINUTES +
  40 MINUTES FREEZING
COOKING TIME: 30 MINUTES
SERVES 4

Wrap the steak in plastic wrap and freeze for 40 minutes. Freezing the meat will make it easier to slice.

Meanwhile, put the onion half, fish sauce, star anise, cinnamon stick, white pepper, stock and 500 ml (17 fl oz/2 cups) water in a large saucepan. Bring to the boil, then reduce the heat, cover and simmer for 20 minutes. Discard the onion, star anise and cinnamon stick.

Put the noodles in a large heatproof bowl. Cover with boiling water and soak for 5 minutes, or until softened. Separate gently and drain. Thinly slice the meat across the grain.

Divide the noodles and spring onion among four deep bowls. Top with the beef, mint, bean sprouts, thinly sliced onion and chilli. Ladle the hot broth over the top and serve with the lemon wedges—the heat of the liquid will cook the beef.

HINTS:
• Fish sauce can be a hidden source of gluten. When you dine out at an Asian restaurant, check that they use a gluten-free fish sauce.
• Some brands of stock (ready-to-use, cubes and powder) are not free of gluten, so check the ingredient list if you are using a commercial brand.
• Vietnamese mint has thin, pointed leaves and a strong peppery, minty flavour. If you can't find it, use regular mint instead.
• People with long-standing coeliac disease often become iron deficient. This soup is a good way to add more iron-rich foods to your diet.

MAIN MEALS

SPICY VEGETABLE STEW WITH DAL

SERVE WITH BASMATI RICE FOR A BALANCED, LOW-GI VEGETARIAN MEAL. THE SPICES ADD COLOUR AND FLAVOUR AND USEFUL AMOUNTS OF MANY MINERALS. BOTH THE DAL AND STEW ARE DELICIOUS REHEATED THE NEXT DAY.

DAL
140 g (5 oz/²/₃ cup) yellow split peas
5 cm (2 in) piece of fresh ginger, grated
2–3 garlic cloves, crushed
1 red chilli, seeded and chopped

3 tomatoes
1 red onion
¼ cauliflower
3 slender eggplants (aubergines)
2 carrots, peeled
2 small zucchini (courgettes)
2 tsp canola or olive oil

1 tsp yellow mustard seeds
1 tsp cumin seeds
1 tsp ground cumin
½ tsp garam masala
375 ml (13 fl oz/1½ cups) vegetable stock GF (Basics)
80 g (2¾ oz/½ cup) frozen peas, thawed
1 large handful coriander (cilantro) leaves

PREP TIME: 25 MINUTES + 2 HOURS SOAKING
COOKING TIME: 1½ HOURS
SERVES 4

To make the dal, put the split peas in a bowl, cover with water and soak for 2 hours. Drain. Put in a large saucepan with the ginger, garlic, chilli and 750 ml (26 fl oz/3 cups) water. Bring to the boil, then reduce the heat and simmer for 40 minutes, or until just soft.

Meanwhile, prepare the vegetables. To peel the tomatoes, score a cross in the base of each one. Cover with boiling water for 30 seconds, then plunge into cold water. Drain and peel away the skin from the cross. Scoop out the seeds with a teaspoon and roughly chop the flesh. Cut the onion into thin wedges, cut the cauliflower into florets and thickly slice the eggplants, carrots and zucchini.

Heat the oil in a large saucepan over medium heat. Add the mustard seeds, cumin seeds, ground cumin and garam masala and cook for 30 seconds, or until fragrant. Add the onion and cook for a further 2 minutes, or until the onion is soft. Stir in the tomato, eggplant, carrot and cauliflower.

Add the dal and stock, mix together well and simmer, covered, for 45 minutes, or until the vegetables are tender. Stir occasionally. Add the zucchini and peas during the last 10 minutes of cooking. Stir in the coriander leaves and serve hot.

nutrition per serve: Energy 858 kJ (204 Cal); Fat 4.3 g; Saturated fat 0.5 g; Protein 14.1 g; Carbohydrate 27.8 g; Fibre 10 g; Cholesterol 0 mg

BEEF AND SPINACH LASAGNE

THIS GLUTEN-FREE VERSION OF LASAGNE CAN BE ENJOYED BY THE WHOLE
FAMILY. THERE'S NO NEED TO COOK SEPARATE VERSIONS FOR THOSE WHO
CAN EAT GLUTEN AND THOSE WHO CAN'T.

1 tbsp canola or olive oil

1 large onion, finely chopped

3 large garlic cloves, crushed

1 celery stalk, diced

500 g (1 lb 2 oz) lean minced (ground) beef

1 tsp dried oregano

2 x 400 g (14 oz) tins diced tomatoes

2 tbsp tomato paste (concentrated purée) GF

250 ml (9 fl oz/1 cup) beef stock GF (Basics)
  or water

500 g (1 lb 2 oz/1 bunch) English spinach,
  stalks removed, washed

375 g (13 oz) gluten-free lasagne sheets

WHITE SAUCE

3 tbsp pure maize cornflour (cornstarch) GF

375 ml (13 fl oz/1½ cups) reduced-fat milk

1 slice of onion

½ tsp ground nutmeg

150 g (5½ oz/⅔ cup) ricotta cheese

90 g (3¼ oz/¾ cup firmly packed) grated
  cheddar cheese GF

PREP TIME: 30 MINUTES

COOKING TIME: 1¾ HOURS

SERVES 6–8

Heat the oil in a large, non-stick saucepan. Add the onion and cook for 2 minutes. Add the
garlic and celery and cook for a further 2 minutes. Add the beef and oregano and cook
over high heat for 5 minutes, or until cooked, breaking up any lumps with a spoon. Add
the tomatoes, tomato paste and stock or water and season with salt and pepper. Reduce
the heat to low and simmer, covered, for 1 hour until reduced and thickened, stirring
occasionally. If the sauce is too thin, remove the lid and simmer until reduced and
thickened. Cool slightly. Cook the spinach with just the water clinging to the leaves in a
covered saucepan for 1 minute, or until wilted.

Meanwhile, to make the white sauce, put the cornflour in a saucepan, add a little of the
milk and mix to a smooth paste. Add the remaining milk, onion slice and nutmeg. Stir
constantly over medium heat until the sauce boils and thickens. Reduce the heat and
simmer for 1 minute. Remove the onion. Stir in the cheeses, then mix until smooth.

Preheat the oven to 180°C (350°F/Gas 4). Arrange one-third of the lasagne sheets over
the base of a 4 litre (140 fl oz/16 cup) rectangular ovenproof dish. Spoon over half the beef,
then cover with half the spinach. Cover with another layer of pasta and spoon over the
remaining beef. Cover with the remaining spinach, then the remaining pasta. Spread over
the white sauce. Bake for 30 minutes, or until golden. Rest for 5 minutes before slicing.

nutrition per serve (8): Energy 1782 kJ (426 Cal); Fat 14.3 g; Saturated fat 6.6 g; Protein 26 g;
Carbohydrate 49 g; Fibre 4.2 g; Cholesterol 57 mg

THREE BEAN CHILLI WITH RICE

2 tsp canola or olive oil

1 large onion, finely chopped

3 garlic cloves, crushed

2 tbsp ground cumin

1 tbsp ground coriander

1 tsp ground cinnamon

1 tsp chilli powder

400 g (14 oz) tin diced tomatoes

375 ml (13 fl oz/1½ cups) vegetable
stock GF (Basics)

400 g (14 oz) tin chickpeas GF, drained and
rinsed

400 g (14 oz) tin red kidney beans GF,
drained and rinsed

400 g (14 oz) tin cannellini (white)
beans GF, drained and rinsed

2 tbsp tomato paste (concentrated
purée) GF

2 tsp sugar

400 g (14 oz/2 cups) basmati rice, rinsed
and drained

PREP TIME: 20 MINUTES

COOKING TIME: 35 MINUTES

SERVES 4

Heat the oil in a large frying pan and cook the onion over medium–low heat for 5 minutes,
or until golden, stirring frequently. Reduce the heat, add the garlic, cumin, coriander,
cinnamon and chilli powder, then stir for 1 minute.

Add the tomatoes, stock, chickpeas, kidney beans and cannellini beans and combine with
the onion mixture. Bring to the boil, then simmer for 20 minutes, stirring occasionally. Add
the tomato paste and sugar and season to taste with salt and freshly ground black pepper.
Simmer for a further 5 minutes.

Meanwhile, put the rice and 1 litre (35 fl oz/4 cups) water in a saucepan and bring to the
boil over medium heat. Reduce the heat to low, cover with a lid and cook for 20 minutes,
or until the rice is tender. Remove from the heat and leave to stand, covered, for 5 minutes.
Serve with the bean chilli.

HINTS:
• It's a good idea to check the label of tinned beans to ensure the manufacturer has not
  used additives or preservatives that contain gluten.
• Top the dish with a little yoghurt or grated cheddar cheese, if you like; if you use
  pre-grated cheddar cheese, check the packet to make sure it doesn't contain gluten.

THIS VEGETARIAN MEAL IS A
GREAT CHOICE FOR PEOPLE WITH
DIABETES OR A HIGH BLOOD
CHOLESTEROL LEVEL—IT'S LOW
GI, LOW IN FAT AND HIGH IN
SOLUBLE FIBRE.

nutrition per serve Energy 2927 kJ (697 Cal)
Fat 7.4 g
Saturated fat 0.9 g
Protein 30.4 g
Carbohydrate 129.4 g
Fibre 21.9 g
Cholesterol 0 mg

87

TUNA KEBABS WITH CHICKPEA TOMATO SALSA

THIS IS A FILLING, LOW-GI MEAL THAT PROVIDES SOME HEALTHY OMEGA-3 FAT (GOOD FOR THE HEART, BRAIN AND EYES, AND FOR REDUCING INFLAMMATION).

SALSA

2 tsp olive oil

2–3 small red chillies, seeded and finely
  chopped

3–4 garlic cloves, crushed

1 red onion, finely chopped

3 tomatoes, seeded and chopped

3 tbsp dry white wine or water

2 x 300 g (10½ oz) tins chickpeas GF,
  drained and rinsed

3 tbsp chopped oregano

4 tbsp chopped parsley

1 kg (2 lb 4 oz) tuna fillet

canola or olive oil spray

lemon wedges, to serve

PREP TIME: 20 MINUTES

COOKING TIME: 20 MINUTES

SERVES 4

To make the salsa, heat the oil in a large saucepan, add the chilli, garlic and onion and stir for 5 minutes, or until softened. Add the tomato and wine or water. Cook over low heat for 10 minutes, or until the mixture is soft, pulpy and the liquid has evaporated. Stir in the chickpeas, oregano and parsley. Season with salt and freshly ground black pepper.

Meanwhile, trim the tuna and cut into 4 cm (1½ in) cubes. Heat a chargrill pan or barbecue hotplate. Thread the tuna onto eight metal skewers, lightly spray with the oil, then cook, turning, for 3 minutes. Do not overcook or the tuna will fall apart. Serve with the salsa and lemon wedges.

HINTS:
• If you are using wooden skewers, soak them in water for 30 minutes before use.
• Check the tin of chickpeas to ensure no gluten-containing ingredients have been added.

nutrition per serve: Energy 2244 kJ (534 Cal); Fat 20 g; Saturated fat 6.6 g; Protein 70.6 g; Carbohydrate 17 g; Fibre 7.7 g; Cholesterol 90 mg

CHILLI CON POLLO

THIS EASY RECIPE IS THE CHICKEN LOVER'S VERSION OF CHILLI CON CARNE.
IF YOU PREFER, YOU CAN MAKE THE MEATIER VERSION BY REPLACING THE
CHICKEN MINCE WITH AN EQUAL WEIGHT OF LEAN BEEF MINCE.

2 tsp olive oil

1 onion, finely chopped

500 g (1 lb 2 oz) lean minced (ground)
  chicken

1–2 tsp mild chilli powder

400 g (14 oz) tin diced tomatoes

2 tbsp tomato paste (concentrated
  purée) GF

400 g (14 oz) tin red kidney beans GF,
  drained and rinsed

400 g (14 oz/2 cups) basmati rice, drained
  and rinsed

4 tbsp chopped parsley

250 g (9 oz/1 cup) low-fat plain yoghurt

PREP TIME: 10 MINUTES

COOKING TIME: 1 HOUR

SERVES 4

Heat the oil in a large saucepan. Add the onion and cook over medium heat for 3 minutes,
or until soft. Increase the heat and add the chicken. Cook until browned, breaking up any
lumps with a wooden spoon.

Add the chilli powder and cook for 1 minute. Add the tomato, tomato paste and 125 ml
(4 fl oz/½ cup) water and stir well. Bring to the boil, then reduce the heat and simmer
for 30 minutes. Stir in the kidney beans and heat through. Season to taste with salt and
freshly ground black pepper.

Meanwhile, put the rice and 1 litre (35 fl oz/4 cups) water in a saucepan and bring to the
boil over medium heat. Reduce the heat to low, cover with a lid and cook for 20 minutes,
or until the rice is tender. Remove from the heat and leave to stand, covered, for 5 minutes.

Sprinkle the chilli con pollo with the parsley and serve with the yoghurt and rice.

HINTS:
• Many people with long-standing untreated coeliac disease become iron deficient. If this
  applies to you, make the recipe with beef mince to increase your iron stores.
• When using tinned beans always check the ingredient list to ensure no additives or
  preservatives that contain gluten have been added.

nutrition per serve: Energy 2871 kJ (683 Cal); Fat 13.8 g; Saturated fat 3.6 g; Protein 40.3 g;
Carbohydrate 98 g; Fibre 7.5 g; Cholesterol 116 mg

IT'S WORTH THE EFFORT IT TAKES
TO COOK THIS HEARTY DISH
BECAUSE THE RESULT IS SO
DELICIOUS. THE VARIETY OF FOODS
IN THIS MEAL MAKES IT HIGHLY
NUTRITIOUS—IT'S A GREAT
SOURCE OF FOLATE, FIBRE AND
VARIOUS ANTIOXIDANTS.

nutrition per serve   Energy 1531 kJ (366 Cal)
Fat 5.2 g
Saturated fat 0.9 g
Protein 17.6 g
Carbohydrate 57.1 g
Fibre 11.6 g
Cholesterol 0 mg

VEGETARIAN PAELLA

200 g (7 oz/1 cup) dried haricot beans

¼ tsp saffron threads

2 tsp olive oil

1 onion, diced

1 red capsicum (pepper), cut into thin strips

5 garlic cloves, crushed

275 g (9¾ oz/1¼ cups) paella or arborio rice

1 tbsp sweet paprika

½ tsp mixed spice

750 ml (26 fl oz/3 cups) vegetable stock GF (Basics)

400 g (14 oz) tin diced tomatoes

1½ tbsp tomato paste (concentrated purée) GF

140 g (5 oz/2⅓ cups) fresh or frozen soya beans

100 g (3½ oz) silverbeet (Swiss chard), shredded

400 g (14 oz) tin artichoke hearts in brine, drained and rinsed

4 tbsp chopped coriander (cilantro) leaves

PREP TIME: 20 MINUTES + OVERNIGHT SOAKING

COOKING TIME: 40 MINUTES

SERVES 6

Put the haricot beans in a large bowl, cover with cold water and leave to soak overnight. Drain and rinse well.

Place the saffron threads in a small frying pan over medium–low heat. Dry-fry, shaking for 1 minute, or until darkened. Remove from the heat and, when cool, crumble into a small bowl. Pour in 125 ml (4 fl oz/½ cup) warm water and allow to steep.

Heat the oil in a large paella pan or frying pan. Add the onion and capsicum and cook over medium–high heat for 5 minutes, or until the onion softens. Stir in the garlic and cook for 1 minute. Reduce the heat and add the drained beans, rice, paprika, mixed spice and season with salt. Stir to coat. Add the saffron water, stock, tomatoes and tomato paste and bring to the boil. Cover, reduce the heat and simmer for 20 minutes.

Stir in the soya beans, silverbeet and artichoke hearts and cook, covered, for 8 minutes, or until all the liquid is absorbed and the rice and beans are tender. Turn off the heat and leave for 5 minutes. Stir in the coriander just before serving.

HINTS:
• Always check the label of commercial stocks to ensure there are no ingredients that contain gluten. Better yet, make your own.
• Top with some grated cheese or plain yoghurt for extra calcium—if you're using pre-grated cheese, make sure no flour has been added by the manufacturer.

HUNGARIAN-STYLE PORK AND LENTIL STEW

THIS MEAL IS LOW IN FAT, LOW GI, AND A GOOD SOURCE OF IRON, ZINC AND B-GROUP VITAMINS, INCLUDING VITAMIN B12.

2 tsp olive oil

2 onions, chopped

500 g (1 lb 2 oz) lean diced pork

2 tsp sweet paprika

1 tsp hot paprika

½ tsp dried thyme

2 tbsp tomato paste (concentrated purée) GF

1 tsp soft brown sugar

3 tbsp red lentils

375 ml (13 fl oz/1½ cups) beef stock GF
   (Basics)

1 tomato

400 g (14 oz/2 cups) basmati rice, rinsed
   and drained

2 tbsp low-fat plain yoghurt

PREP TIME: 20 MINUTES

COOKING TIME: 1 HOUR 5 MINUTES

SERVES 4

Heat the olive oil in a large, deep saucepan over high heat. Add the onion, pork and paprika and stir for 3–4 minutes, or until browned.

Add the thyme, tomato paste, sugar, lentils and stock and season with salt and freshly ground black pepper. Bring to the boil, reduce the heat to very low and cook, covered, for 20 minutes, stirring occasionally to prevent sticking. Uncover and cook for 15–20 minutes, or until thickened.

Remove from the heat and set aside for 10 minutes. To prepare the tomato, cut it in half and scoop out the seeds. Slice the flesh into thin strips.

Meanwhile, put the rice and 1 litre (35 fl oz/4 cups) water in a saucepan and bring to the boil over medium heat. Reduce the heat to low, cover with a lid and cook for 20 minutes, or until the rice is tender. Remove from the heat and leave to stand, covered, for 5 minutes. Just before serving, stir the yoghurt into the stew. Scatter with tomato. Serve with the rice and a salad.

HINT:
• If you have diabetes and you want to serve this stew with gluten-free pasta or noodles instead of basmati rice, choose a gluten-free pasta with a lower GI, such as a soy-based pasta, or serve with fresh rice noodles.

nutrition per serve: Energy 2485 kJ (592 Cal); Fat 6.5 g; Saturated fat 1.6 g; Protein 41.1 g; Carbohydrate 91.8 g; Fibre 5.1 g; Cholesterol 119 mg

LAMB CASSEROLE WITH BEANS

THIS CASSEROLE MAKES A GREAT MEAL ON A COLD WINTER'S NIGHT—IT'S
WARM AND NOURISHING. COOK DOUBLE PORTIONS SO YOU CAN FREEZE THE
LEFTOVERS TO USE AS QUICK WEEKDAY MEALS.

300 g (10½ oz/1½ cups) dried borlotti or
    red kidney beans
1 kg (2 lb 4 oz) lean boned leg of lamb
2 tsp olive oil
50 g (1¾ oz) low-fat bacon slices GF,
    chopped
1 large onion, chopped
2 garlic cloves, crushed
1 large carrot, peeled and chopped
500 ml (17 fl oz/2 cups) red wine
1 tbsp tomato paste (concentrated purée) GF

375 ml (13 fl oz/1½ cups) beef stock GF
    (Basics)
2 large sprigs of rosemary
2 sprigs of thyme

PREP TIME: 25 MINUTES +
    OVERNIGHT SOAKING
COOKING TIME: 2¼ HOURS
SERVES 6

Put the beans in a large bowl, cover with water and leave to soak overnight. Drain well.

Preheat the oven to 160°C (315°F/Gas 2–3). Trim any fat from the lamb and cut into
bite-sized cubes.

Heat the oil in a large flameproof casserole dish over high heat and brown the lamb in two
batches for 2 minutes. Remove all the lamb from the dish and set aside. Add the bacon
and onion to the casserole dish. Cook over medium heat for 3 minutes, or until the onion
is soft. Add the garlic and carrot and cook for 1 minute, or until fragrant.

Return the lamb and any juices to the pan, increase the heat to high and add the wine.
Bring to the boil and cook for 2 minutes. Add the beans, tomato paste, stock, rosemary
and thyme, bring to the boil, then cover and cook in the oven for 2 hours, or until the meat
is tender. Stir occasionally during cooking and skim off any fat from the surface. Season
with salt and freshly ground black pepper and remove the herb sprigs before serving.

HINTS:
• Serve with some gluten-free pasta or bread.
• Gluten can be a hidden additive in many foods, such as bacon, tomato paste and stock.
  Always check the labels carefully.

nutrition per serve: Energy 1933 kJ (460 Cal); Fat 13.1 g; Saturated fat 5.3 g; Protein 51 g;
Carbohydrate 23 g; Fibre 10.7 g; Cholesterol 113 mg

HERB-CRUSTED LAMB ROAST WITH VEGETABLES

6 large carrots, peeled and cut into 2 cm
(¾ in) pieces on the diagonal
canola or olive oil spray
2 tbsp Dijon mustard GF
2 tbsp finely chopped flat-leaf (Italian)
parsley
1 tsp finely chopped thyme
1 tsp finely chopped sage
3 garlic cloves, crushed
2 x 300 g (10½ oz) pieces lamb rump or
mini lamb roasts, trimmed

750 g (1 lb 10 oz) small new potatoes
250 ml (9 fl oz/1 cup) vegetable stock GF
(Basics)
625 g (1 lb 6 oz/4 cups) frozen peas,
thawed
2 tbsp mint

PREP TIME: 20 MINUTES
COOKING TIME: 1 HOUR
SERVES 4

Preheat the oven to 200°C (400°F/Gas 6). Spray the carrots with the oil, season well and place into a large roasting tin (you will be adding the lamb pieces halfway through cooking). Cook in the oven for 1 hour, or until golden and soft.

Place the mustard, parsley, thyme, sage and 2 of the crushed garlic cloves in a bowl. Mix well to combine and add the lamb pieces. Thoroughly coat with the mixture and add to the carrots in the roasting tin 30 minutes before it is due to be ready.

Meanwhile, cook the new potatoes in a large saucepan of boiling water for 12 minutes, or until tender. Drain.

In a small saucepan over high heat, bring the vegetable stock to the boil with the remaining crushed garlic clove. Add the peas and cook for 3 minutes. Remove from the heat and strain, reserving the stock. Put the peas, mint and reserved stock in a food processor. Blend until smooth, then season to taste.

Remove the lamb from the oven and allow to rest, covered, on a board for 5 minutes before slicing across the grain. Divide among four plates and serve with the boiled potatoes, pea and mint purée and roasted carrots.

HINT:
• You should be able to find a gluten-free mustard in the supermarket—just check the label.

CANCEL YOUR DINNER RESERVATIONS—YOU CAN ENJOY THIS RESTAURANT-STYLE FOOD AT HOME WITHOUT HAVING TO CHECK IF IT'S FREE OF GLUTEN. SERVE IT TO FAMILY AND FRIENDS.

nutrition per serve   Energy 2006 kJ (479 Cal)
Fat 8.4 g
Saturated fat 2.7 g
Protein 45.5 g
Carbohydrate 46.7 g
Fibre 16.5 g
Cholesterol 102 g

CHICKEN WITH SNOW PEAS, SPROUTS AND NOODLES

THIS QUICK GLUTEN-FREE MEAL IS A GREAT RECIPE TO ADD TO YOUR COLLECTION OF FAVOURITE WEEKDAY RECIPES. IT TAKES LITTLE TIME TO PREPARE AND COOK AND GIVES YOU A NUTRITIOUS, FILLING MEAL.

300 g (10½ oz) dried mung bean vermicelli
500 g (1 lb 2 oz) boneless, skinless chicken
  breast
2 tsp canola or olive oil
1 onion, thinly sliced
3 makrut (kaffir lime) leaves, shredded
1 red capsicum (pepper), sliced
70 g (2½ oz) snow peas (mangetout),
  trimmed
3 tbsp lime juice
100 ml (3½ fl oz) tamari GF

50 g (1¾ oz) snow pea (mangetout)
  sprouts, trimmed
2 tbsp chopped coriander (cilantro) leaves

PREP TIME: 15 MINUTES +
  10 MINUTES SOAKING
COOKING TIME: 30 MINUTES
SERVES 4

Put the noodles in a large bowl and cover with warm water. Soak for 10 minutes, or until they are translucent. Drain. Transfer to a saucepan of boiling water and cook for 10 minutes, or until tender. Rinse under cold water and drain.

Meanwhile, trim the chicken and cut into thin slices. Heat a wok over medium heat, add the oil and swirl to coat. Add the onion and kaffir lime leaves and stir-fry for 3–5 minutes, or until the onion begins to soften. Remove from the wok. Add the chicken in batches and cook for a further 4 minutes, or until lightly browned. Remove from the wok and set aside. Reheat the wok between batches.

Return the onion mixture and all the chicken to the wok, add the capsicum and snow peas and continue to cook for 2–3 minutes. Stir in the lime juice, tamari and 2 tablespoons water and cook for 1–2 minutes, or until the sauce reduces slightly. Add the noodles and toss through the mixture to warm through. Add the sprouts and coriander and cook until the sprouts have wilted slightly.

HINT:
• Use the chicken, tamari and lime juice as a base, then add vegetables and herbs to taste. For example, use asparagus instead of snow peas, or mint instead of coriander.

nutrition per serve: Energy 2116 kJ (505 Cal); Fat 9.3 g; Saturated fat 2.3 g; Protein 30.9 g; Carbohydrate 71.3 g; Fibre 2.1 g; Cholesterol 82 mg

MIXED BEANS AND CAPSICUM STIR-FRY

THIS DISH TAKES LESS THAN 30 MINUTES TO MAKE AND CAN BE SERVED AS A SIDE DISH OR AS A VEGETARIAN MAIN MEAL. IT'S LOW GI AND RICH IN FIBRE, ANTIOXIDANTS AND FOLATE.

2 tsp canola or olive oil
2 garlic cloves, crushed
1 red onion, cut into thin wedges
1 red capsicum (pepper), cut into short, thin strips
1 yellow capsicum (pepper), cut into short, thin strips
400 g (14 oz) tin chickpeas GF, drained and rinsed
400 g (14 oz) tin red kidney beans GF, drained and rinsed

1 tsp soft brown sugar
2 tbsp balsamic vinegar
3 tbsp lime juice
250 g (9 oz) cherry tomatoes, halved
1 Lebanese (short) cucumber, chopped
3 tbsp chopped coriander (cilantro) leaves
butter lettuce leaves, to serve

PREP TIME: 15 MINUTES
COOKING TIME: 10 MINUTES
SERVES 6

Heat a wok until very hot, add the oil and swirl to coat. Add the garlic, onion and red and yellow capsicum strips and stir-fry over medium heat for 2–3 minutes. Remove from the wok and set aside.

Add the chickpeas and kidney beans to the wok, stir in the brown sugar and balsamic vinegar and toss for 2–3 minutes, or until the liquid has reduced by half. Add the lime juice and toss until well combined.

Using two wooden spoons, stir in the cherry tomatoes, cucumber, coriander and the onion and capsicum mixture. Stir-fry briefly until heated through and thoroughly mixed. Put a couple of lettuce leaves on each plate and spoon the stir-fry onto the leaves to serve.

HINTS:
• Even though most tinned legumes don't contain gluten it's a good idea to check the ingredient list to ensure the manufacturer has not added any gluten-containing additives or preservatives.
• Serve the stir-fry with basmati rice or quinoa instead of lettuce leaves for a more balanced low-GI vegetarian meal.

nutrition per serve: Energy 478 kJ (114 Cal); Fat 2.8 g; Saturated fat 0.3 g; Protein 6.4 g; Carbohydrate 15.3 g; Fibre 6.1 g; Cholesterol 0 mg

IF YOU CAN'T BE SURE THAT YOUR
LOCAL INDIAN RESTAURANT HAS
GLUTEN-FREE DISHES AVAILABLE,
THEN A HOME-MADE CURRY IS THE
SAFEST OPTION. THIS LAMB CURRY
IS A GOOD SOURCE OF IRON, ZINC
AND B-GROUP VITAMINS.

nutrition per serve Energy 2330 kJ (555 Cal)

Fat 15.2 g

Saturated fat 5.3 g

Protein 44.6 g

Carbohydrate 59.5 g

Fibre 3.4 g

Cholesterol 114 mg

ROGAN JOSH

1 kg (2 lb 4 oz) lean boned leg of lamb
2 tsp canola or olive oil
2 onions, chopped
125 g (4½ oz/½ cup) low-fat plain
 yoghurt
1 tsp chilli powder
1 tbsp ground coriander
2 tsp ground cumin
1 tsp ground cardamom
1 tsp ground turmeric
½ tsp ground cloves
3 garlic cloves, crushed
1 tbsp grated fresh ginger

400 g (14 oz) tin diced tomatoes
1 tsp salt
3 tbsp slivered almonds
400 g (14 oz/2 cups) basmati rice, rinsed
 and drained
1 tsp garam masala
chopped coriander (cilantro) leaves,
 to serve

PREP TIME: 25 MINUTES
COOKING TIME: 2 HOURS
SERVES 6

Trim the lamb of any fat or sinew and cut into small cubes. Heat the oil in a large heavy-based saucepan, add the onion and cook, stirring, for 5 minutes, or until soft. Stir in the yoghurt, chilli powder, coriander, cumin, cardamom, turmeric, cloves, garlic and ginger. Add the tomato and salt and simmer for 5 minutes.

Add the lamb and stir until coated. Cover and cook over low heat, stirring occasionally, for 1–1½ hours, or until the lamb is tender. Uncover and simmer until the liquid thickens.

Meanwhile, toast the almonds in a dry frying pan over medium heat for 3–4 minutes, shaking the pan gently, until the nuts are golden brown. Remove from the pan at once to prevent them burning. Put the rice and 1 litre (35 fl oz/4 cups) water in a saucepan and bring to the boil over medium heat. Reduce the heat to low, cover with a lid and cook for 20 minutes, or until the rice is tender. Remove from the heat and leave to stand, covered, for 5 minutes.

Add the garam masala to the curry and mix through well. Sprinkle the slivered almonds and coriander leaves over the top and serve with the rice.

HINTS:
• This curry is delicious served the next day, after the flavours have had time to develop more fully.
• Serve with plain gluten-free poppadoms—cook them in a microwave, so they contain less fat and are ready in a flash. Other traditional Indian side dishes also make refreshing accompaniments to this meal (such as cucumber raita, tomato and onions, and bananas in lemon juice and desiccated coconut).

TANDOORI FISH CUTLETS

THE SPICES ADD COLOUR, FLAVOUR AND VALUABLE MINERALS TO THIS
LOW-GI DISH. MARINATING THE FISH OVERNIGHT SAVES PREPARATION TIME
THE NEXT DAY.

4 firm white fish cutlets
3 tbsp lemon juice
1 onion, finely chopped
2 garlic cloves, crushed
1 tbsp grated fresh ginger
1 red chilli
1 tbsp garam masala
1 tsp paprika
¼ tsp salt

500 g (1 lb 2 oz/2 cups) low-fat plain
   yoghurt
400 g (14 oz/2 cups) basmati rice, rinsed
   and drained

PREP TIME: 20 MINUTES +
   OVERNIGHT MARINATING
COOKING TIME: 30 MINUTES
SERVES 4

Pat the fish cutlets dry with paper towels and arrange in a shallow non-metallic dish.
Drizzle the lemon juice over the fish and turn to coat the cutlets with the juice.

To make the marinade, blend the onion, garlic, ginger, chilli, garam masala, paprika and salt
in a blender until smooth. Transfer to a bowl and stir in the yoghurt. Spoon the marinade
over the fish and turn the fish to coat thoroughly. Cover and refrigerate overnight.

Put the rice and 1 litre (35 fl oz/4 cups) water in a saucepan and bring to the boil over
medium heat. Reduce the heat to low, cover with a lid and cook for 20 minutes, or until
the rice is tender. Remove from the heat and leave to stand, covered, for 5 minutes.

Meanwhile, heat a grill (broiler) or barbecue hotplate. Remove the cutlets from the
marinade and allow any excess to drip off. Cook the cutlets under the grill or on the
barbecue for 3–4 minutes on each side, or until the fish flakes easily when tested with
a fork. Serve with the rice.

HINTS:
• Try blue eye, snapper or warehou.
• This is delicious served with extra yoghurt and baby English spinach leaves or a cooling
   cucumber raita.

nutrition per serve: Energy 2743 kJ (653 Cal); Fat 8.2 g; Saturated fat 4.1 g; Protein 53.9 g;
Carbohydrate 89 g; Fibre 2.7 g; Cholesterol 142 mg

CORIANDER BEEF WITH NOODLES

THIS IS THE PERFECT RECIPE FOR A QUICK WEEKDAY MEAL. MARINATE
THE MEAT OVERNIGHT, SO ALL YOU HAVE TO DO THE NEXT DAY IS QUICKLY
PREPARE THE REST OF THE INGREDIENTS, THEN STIR-FRY.

4 garlic cloves, finely chopped
1 tbsp finely chopped fresh ginger
1 large handful coriander (cilantro) roots,
   stems and leaves, chopped
3 tsp canola or olive oil
500 g (1 lb 2 oz) lean beef rump steak
400 g (14 oz) fresh rice noodles
1 red onion, thinly sliced
½ red capsicum (pepper), thinly sliced
½ green capsicum (pepper), thinly sliced

2 tbsp lime juice
2 tbsp tamari GF
1 large handful coriander (cilantro) leaves,
   extra

PREP TIME: 20 MINUTES +
   2 HOURS MARINATING
COOKING TIME: 20 MINUTES
SERVES 4

To make the marinade, combine the garlic, ginger, coriander and 2 teaspoons of the oil
in a large non-metallic bowl. Trim the beef, then cut into thin strips across the grain.
Add to the marinade and toss to coat. Cover with plastic wrap and refrigerate for 2 hours
or overnight.

Put the rice noodles in a large heatproof bowl, cover with boiling water and soak for
8 minutes, or until softened. Separate gently and drain.

Heat a wok until very hot and spray with canola or olive oil. Add the meat in three batches
and stir-fry for 2–3 minutes, or until the meat is just cooked. Remove all the meat from the
wok and keep it warm. Reheat and respray the wok between batches.

Heat the remaining 1 teaspoon oil in the wok, add the onion and cook over medium heat
for 3–4 minutes, or until slightly softened. Add the capsicum slices and cook, tossing
constantly, for a further 3–4 minutes, or until slightly softened.

Return all the meat to the wok along with the lime juice, tamari, 2 tablespoons water and
extra coriander. Add the noodles. Toss well, then remove from the heat and season well
with salt and freshly ground black pepper.

HINT:
• Tamari is usually wheat free but check the label to ensure it is gluten free.

nutrition per serve: Energy 1701 kJ (406 Cal); Fat 10 g; Saturated fat 2.8 g; Protein 32.6 g;
Carbohydrate 44.3 g; Fibre 2.2 g; Cholesterol 80 mg

GREEK-STYLE CALAMARI

STUFFING

2 tsp olive oil

2 spring onions (scallions), sliced

280 g (10 oz/1½ cups) cold, cooked
basmati rice

4 tbsp pine nuts

4 tbsp finely chopped dried apricots

2 tbsp chopped parsley

2 tsp finely grated lemon zest

1 egg, lightly beaten

1 kg (2 lb 4 oz) cleaned squid tubes

SAUCE

4 large ripe tomatoes

2 tsp olive oil

1 onion, finely chopped

1 garlic clove, crushed

3 tbsp good-quality red wine

1 tbsp chopped oregano

PREP TIME: 30 MINUTES

COOKING TIME: 35 MINUTES

SERVES 4–6

Preheat the oven to 160°C (315°F/Gas 2–3). To make the stuffing, mix together the oil, spring onion, rice, pine nuts, apricots, parsley and lemon zest in a bowl. Add enough egg to moisten all the ingredients.

Wash the squid tubes and pat dry inside and out with paper towels. Three-quarters fill each squid tube with the stuffing. Secure the ends with toothpicks or skewers. Place in a single layer in a casserole dish.

To make the sauce, begin by peeling the tomatoes. Score a cross in the base of each one. Cover with boiling water for 30 seconds, then plunge into cold water. Drain and peel away the tomato skin from the cross. Chop the flesh. Heat the oil in a frying pan. Add the onion and garlic and cook over low heat for 2 minutes, or until the onion is soft. Add the tomato, wine and oregano and bring to the boil. Reduce the heat, cover with a lid and cook over low heat for 10 minutes.

Pour the hot sauce over the squid, cover and bake for 20 minutes, or until the squid is tender. Remove the toothpicks before cutting into thick slices for serving. Spoon the sauce over just before serving.

HINT:
• You will need to cook 100 g (3½ oz/½ cup) raw basmati rice for this recipe.

TAKE A TRIP TO THE COAST OF
THE MEDITERRANEAN WITH THIS
TASTY DISH. IT'S MUCH MORE
NUTRITIOUS THAN DEEP-FRIED
COMMERCIAL CALAMARI—IT'S LOW
GI AND PROVIDES GOOD AMOUNTS
OF THE MINERALS IRON, ZINC,
IODINE AND SELENIUM.

nutrition per serve (6)   Energy 1454 kJ (346 Cal)
Fat 13.2 g
Saturated fat 1.8 g
Protein 33.4 g
Carbohydrate 21.7 g
Fibre 3.9 g
Cholesterol 363 mg

SPRING VEGETABLE RISOTTO

WELCOME THE RETURN OF SPRING WITH THIS DELICIOUS RISOTTO. YOU CAN STIR IN SOME FRESHLY COOKED CHICKEN PIECES BEFORE SERVING FOR A MORE SUBSTANTIAL MEAL WITH MORE PROTEIN, IRON AND ZINC.

250 g (9 oz) cherry tomatoes

3 unpeeled garlic cloves

3 sprigs of thyme

canola or olive oil spray

1.75 litres (61 fl oz/7 cups) chicken or vegetable stock GF (Basics)

2 tsp olive oil

1 onion, finely chopped

440 g (15½ oz/2 cups) arborio rice

175 g (6 oz) asparagus, trimmed and cut into 2 cm (¾ in) pieces

175 g (6 oz) baby carrots, halved on the diagonal

115 g (4 oz/¾ cup) frozen peas, thawed

2 tbsp chopped mint

2 tbsp chopped basil

2 tbsp chopped flat-leaf (Italian) parsley

4 tbsp freshly grated parmesan cheese

PREP TIME: 20 MINUTES

COOKING TIME: 30 MINUTES

SERVES 4

Preheat the oven to 180°C (350°F/Gas 4). Toss the tomatoes in a glass or ceramic ovenproof dish with the unpeeled garlic cloves and thyme. Spray with the oil. Season with salt and freshly ground black pepper, then bake, uncovered, for 30 minutes, or until the tomatoes are soft but still whole.

Meanwhile, pour the stock into a saucepan and bring to the boil. Reduce the heat and keep the stock at a gentle simmer. Heat the oil in a heavy-based saucepan over medium heat, add the onion and cook, stirring, for 6–7 minutes, or until the onion has softened. Add the rice and stir through for 1 minute, or until well coated.

Add 125 ml (4 fl oz/½ cup) of the hot stock. Cook over medium heat, stirring constantly, until most of the stock has been absorbed. Continue adding the stock, 125 ml (4 fl oz/ ½ cup) at a time, stirring constantly. After 15 minutes, add the asparagus and carrot, then continue adding the remaining stock until it has all been absorbed and the rice is creamy and tender. Stir through the peas, herbs and parmesan. Season to taste.

Serve the risotto in individual serving bowls topped with the roasted cherry tomatoes and drizzled with any juices from the cooked tomatoes.

nutrition per serve: Energy 2315 kJ (553 Cal); Fat 6.8 g; Saturated fat 2.3 g; Protein 17.7 g; Carbohydrate 100.8 g; Fibre 7.9 g; Cholesterol 26 mg

CRUNCHY COATED CHICKEN

IF YOU MISS REGULAR BATTERED OR CRUMBED FRIED CHICKEN, THEN THIS RECIPE IS FOR YOU: IT'S A LOWER FAT, GLUTEN-FREE VERSION. IT CAN BE SERVED WARM OR COLD AND MAKES A GOOD ADDITION TO A PICNIC HAMPER.

80 g (2¾ oz/½ cup) gluten-free plain
  (all-purpose) flour
2 eggs
90 g (3¼ oz/1 cup) rice bran
2–3 tbsp poppy seeds
10 (2 kg/4 lb 8 oz) chicken pieces,
  skin removed
canola or olive oil spray

CHIVE YOGHURT
125 g (4½ oz/½ cup) low-fat plain
  yoghurt GF
2 tbsp snipped chives

PREP TIME: 20 MINUTES +
  30 MINUTES REFRIGERATION
COOKING TIME: 30 MINUTES
SERVES 4

Preheat the oven to 200°C (400°F/Gas 6). Lightly grease a baking tray.

Put the flour in a shallow bowl. Mix the eggs with 2 tablespoons water in a separate bowl and mix the bran, poppy seeds and a little salt in a third bowl. Dust the chicken pieces lightly with the flour. Dip them in the combined egg and water, then roll in the bran mixture, pressing the mixture on firmly. Put the chicken pieces on the prepared tray and refrigerate for 30 minutes to firm the coating.

Spray the chicken all over with oil spray. Bake for about 30 minutes, or until golden brown and cooked through when tested.

Meanwhile, to make the chive yoghurt, combine the yoghurt and chives in a small bowl, then season to taste with salt.

Serve the chicken hot or cold with the chive yoghurt.

HINT:
• Serve with a salad and potato wedges.

nutrition per serve: Energy 2687 kJ (642 Cal); Fat 27.1 g; Saturated fat 6.5 g; Protein 66.9 g; Carbohydrate 27.9 g; Fibre 8.1 g; Cholesterol 313 mg

THIS COLOURFUL MEAL IS FULL
OF THE FLAVOURS OF THE
MEDITERRANEAN. IT PROVIDES
GOOD AMOUNTS OF PROTEIN,
IRON, ZINC AND ANTIOXIDANTS.
SERVE WITH RICE, QUINOA,
GLUTEN-FREE PASTA OR BREAD.

nutrition per serve   Energy 1510 kJ (359 Cal)

Fat 12.7 g

Saturated fat 3.5 g

Protein 50.6 g

Carbohydrate 8.6 g

Fibre 5.4 g

Cholesterol 132 mg

CHICKEN WITH BAKED EGGPLANT AND TOMATO

1 red capsicum (pepper)
1 eggplant (aubergine)
3 tomatoes
200 g (7 oz) large button mushrooms
1 onion
canola or olive oil spray
1½ tbsp tomato paste (concentrated purée) GF
125 ml (4 fl oz/½ cup) chicken stock GF (Basics)

3 tbsp dry white wine
2 low-fat bacon slices GF
4 boneless, skinless chicken breasts
4 small sprigs of rosemary

PREP TIME: 30 MINUTES
COOKING TIME: 1½ HOURS
SERVES 4

Preheat the oven to 200°C (400°F/Gas 6). Cut the capsicum and eggplant into bite-sized pieces. Cut the tomatoes into quarters, the mushrooms in half and the onion into thin wedges. Mix the vegetables together in a roasting tin. Spray with the oil and bake for 1 hour, or until starting to brown and soften, stirring once.

Mix together the tomato paste, stock and wine, then pour into the roasting tin and roast the vegetables for a further 10 minutes, or until the sauce has thickened.

Meanwhile, cut the bacon in half lengthways. Wrap a strip around each chicken breast and secure it underneath with a toothpick. Poke a sprig of fresh rosemary underneath the bacon. Heat a non-stick frying pan over medium heat. Spray with the oil. Cook the chicken for 2–3 minutes on each side, or until golden on both sides. Cover and cook for 10–15 minutes, or until the chicken is cooked through. Remove the toothpicks. Serve the chicken on a bed of the vegetables.

HINTS:
• Always check the ingredient list of commercial stocks because they often contain gluten.
• Gluten can be added in the preserving process of meats such as bacon, so check the ingredient list before you buy.

SEAFOOD PASTA

THIS PASTA DISH IS A GREAT CHOICE FOR ACTIVE PEOPLE—A SINGLE SERVE
PROVIDES PLENTY OF CARBOHYDRATE FOR ENERGY AND GOOD AMOUNTS OF
MANY VITAMINS AND MINERALS.

1 tbsp olive oil
1 large onion, cut into thin wedges
2 garlic cloves, crushed
80 g (2¾ oz) button mushrooms, thinly
   sliced
3 ripe tomatoes, roughly chopped
2 x 400 g (14 oz) tins diced tomatoes
1 tbsp tomato paste (concentrated
   purée)GF
1 tsp sugar
1 tsp freshly ground black pepper
3 tbsp capers, rinsed, drained and chopped
8 medium raw prawns (shrimp), peeled
   and deveined

8 scallops, trimmed
2 small cleaned squid tubes, cut into rings
1 large handful flat-leaf (Italian) parsley,
   finely chopped
1 handful basil, shredded
500 g (1 lb 2 oz) gluten-free fettuccine or
   other pasta
freshly grated parmesan cheese, to serve
   (optional)

PREP TIME: 15 MINUTES
COOKING TIME: 30 MINUTES
SERVES 4–6

Heat the olive oil in a large, deep, heavy-based saucepan. Add the onion and garlic and
cook for 2 minutes, or until softened. Add the mushrooms, fresh and tinned tomatoes,
tomato paste, sugar, pepper, capers and 250 ml (9 fl oz/1 cup) water. Bring to the boil,
then reduce the heat and simmer for 20 minutes. Stir in the prawns, scallops and squid,
then cook for a further 2–3 minutes until the seafood is just cooked. Just before serving,
stir in the parsley and basil.

Meanwhile, cook the pasta in a large saucepan of boiling salted water for 10 minutes,
or according to the packet instructions, until just tender. Drain well and return to the
saucepan. Toss through the sauce. Divide into bowls and serve with the grated parmesan
cheese, if you like.

nutrition per serve (6): Energy 1867 kJ (446 Cal); Fat 5.1 g; Saturated fat 0.9 g; Protein 20.6 g;
Carbohydrate 75.8 g; Fibre 6.2 g; Cholesterol 110 mg

GINGER CHILLI FISH CUTLETS WITH CORIANDER RICE

THIS ASIAN-STYLE MEAL IS A GREAT CHOICE FOR PEOPLE WHO ARE WATCHING THEIR WEIGHT.

400 g (14 oz/2 cups) basmati rice, rinsed and drained

4 firm white fish cutlets

5 cm (2 in) piece of fresh ginger, shredded

2 garlic cloves, chopped

2 tsp chopped red chilli

2 tbsp chopped coriander (cilantro) stems and leaves

3 spring onions (scallions), thinly sliced

coriander (cilantro) leaves, chopped, extra

3 tbsp lime juice

1 tbsp fish sauce GF

2 tsp honey

PREP TIME: 20 MINUTES

COOKING TIME: 30 MINUTES

SERVES 4

Put the rice and 1 litre (35 fl oz/4 cups) water in a saucepan and bring to the boil over medium heat. Reduce the heat to low, cover with a lid and cook for 20 minutes, or until the rice is tender. Remove from the heat and leave to stand, covered, for 5 minutes.

Meanwhile, cook the fish. Line a large bamboo steamer basket with baking paper or banana leaves. Arrange the fish in the basket and top with the ginger, garlic, chilli and coriander stems and leaves. Cover with a lid and steam over a wok or large saucepan of boiling water for 8–10 minutes, without letting the basket touch the water. Sprinkle the spring onion over the fish. Cover and steam for a further 30 seconds, or until the fish flakes easily with a fork.

Stir the extra coriander leaves into the rice. Divide the rice onto serving plates. Top with the fish and pour over the combined lime juice, fish sauce and honey.

HINTS:
• Try snapper, jewfish or blue eye.
• There are many brands of gluten-free fish sauce available.

nutrition per serve: Energy 2236 kJ (534 Cal); Fat 3.2 g; Saturated fat 1.1 g; Protein 39.7 g; Carbohydrate 84.1 g; Fibre 1.6 g; Cholesterol 96 mg

RICE-CRUMBED FISH WITH WEDGES

2 eggs
2 tbsp milk
4 tbsp gluten-free plain (all-purpose) flour
80 g (2¾ oz/1 cup) rice crumbs
4 boneless white fish fillets
canola or olive oil spray
lettuce or salad leaves, to serve
chutney GF (Basics), to serve

WEDGES
1 kg (2 lb 4 oz) all-purpose potatoes,
   peeled and cut into wedges
canola or olive oil spray

PREP TIME: 20 MINUTES
COOKING TIME: 50 MINUTES
SERVES 4

Preheat the oven to 220°C (425°F/Gas 7). Line two large baking trays with sheets of baking paper.

Combine the eggs and milk in a shallow bowl. Put the flour in a shallow dish and season with salt and pepper. Put the rice crumbs in a separate shallow dish. Dip the fish in the flour, followed by the egg mixture and, lastly, the rice crumbs. Lay the crumbed fish in a single layer on one of the lined trays. Refrigerate until required.

Put the potato wedges in a large bowl and sprinkle with salt. Spray the wedges with oil, then toss to coat. Spread over the second lined tray.

Bake the potato wedges for 30 minutes, turning once. Put the wedges on the lower shelf of the oven. Remove the fish from the fridge, then spray both sides of the fish lightly with oil. Add the fish to the top shelf and cook for 20 minutes, or until the fish is cooked and the wedges are crispy. Serve the fish with the wedges, lettuce and chutney.

HINT:
• It can be hard to find gluten-free versions of commercially available chutneys, relishes and sauces, so why not make your own instead?

YOU DON'T NEED TO AVOID FISH AND CHIPS WHEN YOU'RE ON A GLUTEN-FREE DIET—JUST MAKE YOUR OWN GLUTEN-FREE VERSION. OVEN-BAKING THE FISH AND CHIPS MAKES THIS VERSION MUCH LOWER IN FAT THAN THE DEEP-FRIED VARIETY.

nutrition per serve   Energy 2058 kJ (492 Cal)

Fat 9.1 g

Saturated fat 2.4 g

Protein 42.7 g

Carbohydrate 56.1 g

Fibre 4 g

Cholesterol 188 mg

111

SIRLOIN STEAKS WITH ROASTED CAPSICUM AND GREEN OLIVE SALAD

IF YOU HAVE AN IRON DEFICIENCY, TRY THIS MEAL. IT'S A GREAT SOURCE OF WELL-ABSORBED IRON AND CAN BE ENJOYED BY THE WHOLE FAMILY.

750 g (1 lb 10 oz) small new potatoes

1 red capsicum (pepper), seeded and quartered

100 g (3½ oz) green beans, trimmed and halved

500 g (1 lb 2 oz) lean sirloin steak, cut into 4 fillets or 4 x 125 g (4½ oz) fillet steaks

250 ml (9 fl oz/1 cup) red wine

2 tbsp balsamic vinegar

1 tbsp soft brown sugar

10 small thyme leaves

4 handfuls mixed salad leaves

90 g (3¼ oz/½ cup) green olives in brine, pitted and lightly squashed

1 tbsp baby capers, rinsed and drained (optional)

PREP TIME: 20 MINUTES

COOKING TIME: 25 MINUTES

SERVES 4

Put the potatoes in a saucepan of boiling water. Cook for 12 minutes, or until tender, then drain, refresh and cut in half. Set aside.

Meanwhile, preheat a grill (broiler) to medium. Roast the capsicum, skin side up, until the skin blackens and blisters. Set aside in a plastic bag for 5 minutes, then peel away the skin and slice the flesh into thin strips. Blanch the beans for 2 minutes in a saucepan of boiling water. Drain and refresh.

Pat the meat dry with paper towels. Lightly brush a non-stick frying pan with oil and heat to very hot. Add the meat and cook for 2–3 minutes on each side, or until cooked to your liking. Remove from the pan, cover with foil and set aside while preparing the sauce.

Add the wine, vinegar, sugar and half of the thyme leaves to the frying pan. Bring to the boil, stirring continuously. Boil until reduced by about one-third. Set aside until just warm.

Toss together the salad leaves, capsicum and beans in a large bowl. Divide the salad leaves equally onto four large plates. Scatter over the potatoes, olives and capers, if using. Cut the fillets into 1 cm (½ in) thick slices and arrange on top of the salad. Drizzle over the dressing and garnish with the remaining thyme leaves.

nutrition per serve: Energy 1706 kJ (407 Cal); Fat 9.5 g; Saturated fat 3.6 g; Protein 31.8 g; Carbohydrate 34.3 g; Fibre 5.8 g; Cholesterol 72 mg

SPAGHETTI BOLOGNESE

THIS GLUTEN-FREE VERSION OF THE TRADITIONAL RECIPE IS A REAL CROWD PLEASER AND IS A GREAT CHOICE FOR A HEALTHY WEEKDAY MEAL. IT IS ALSO DELICIOUS SERVED AS LEFTOVERS THE NEXT DAY.

1 tbsp canola or olive oil
1 onion, chopped
2 large garlic cloves, crushed
1 celery stalk, diced
1 carrot, peeled and diced
90 g (3¼ oz) button mushrooms, finely chopped
500 g (1 lb 2 oz) lean minced (ground) beef
1 tsp dried oregano
250 ml (9 fl oz/1 cup) red wine
250 ml (9 fl oz/1 cup) beef stock GF (Basics)

2 x 400 g (14 oz) tins diced tomatoes
2 tbsp tomato paste (concentrated purée) GF
375 g (13 oz) gluten-free spaghetti
freshly grated parmesan cheese, to serve
2 tbsp chopped basil

PREP TIME: 20 MINUTES
COOKING TIME: 1½ HOURS
SERVES 4

Heat the oil in a large, non-stick saucepan. Add the onion and cook, stirring occasionally, for 3 minutes. Add the garlic, celery, carrot and mushroom and cook for a further 2 minutes. Add the minced beef and cook over high heat for 5 minutes, or until cooked, breaking up any lumps with the back of a spoon. Add the oregano and wine and cook for 3–4 minutes, or until most of the liquid has evaporated.

Add the stock, tomatoes and tomato paste and season with salt and pepper. Reduce the heat to low and simmer, covered, for 1 hour, stirring occasionally to prevent it from catching on the bottom. If the sauce is too thin, remove the lid and simmer until reduced and thickened. Cool slightly.

Meanwhile, cook the spaghetti in a large saucepan of boiling salted water for 10 minutes, or according to the packet instructions, until tender. Drain well. Toss the spaghetti with the sauce and serve with the parmesan and basil.

HINTS:
• You can serve regular or gluten-free spaghetti with this bolognese sauce, if you need to cater for different family members. Just make sure that you cook the two types of pasta in separate saucepans and drain in separate colanders.
• Serve with a mixed leaf salad dressed with balsamic vinegar.

nutrition per serve: Energy 2735 kJ (653 Cal); Fat 14.7 g; Saturated fat 4.2 g; Protein 35.4 g; Carbohydrate 78.6 g; Fibre 6.5 g; Cholesterol 64 mg

BORED WITH REGULAR ROAST CHICKEN? TRY THIS VERSION FOR A CHANGE. SERVE WITH A VARIETY OF STEAMED VEGETABLES FOR A SATISFYING MEAL. REMEMBER TO TAKE THE SKIN OFF THE CHICKEN BEFORE YOU EAT IT, IF YOU'RE WATCHING YOUR WEIGHT.

nutrition per serve Energy 2525 kJ (603 Cal)
Fat 38.6 g
Saturated fat 12.6 g
Protein 45.7 g
Carbohydrate 19 g
Fibre 0.5 g
Cholesterol 245 mg

114

ROAST CHICKEN WITH STUFFING

1.5 kg (3 lb 5 oz) whole chicken
2 tsp canola or olive oil
1 tbsp golden syrup or honey

PUMPKIN AND BREADCRUMB STUFFING
10 g (¼ oz) butter
2 spring onions (scallions), thinly sliced
1 garlic clove, crushed

80 g (2¾ oz/1 cup) fresh gluten-free
   breadcrumbs
60 g (2¼ oz/½ cup) finely grated butternut
   pumpkin (squash)

PREP TIME: 30 MINUTES
COOKING TIME: 1½ HOURS
SERVES 4

Preheat the oven to 180°C (350°F/Gas 4). Lightly oil a roasting tin. To prepare the chicken, remove the neck, rinse out the cavity with cold water and pat dry with paper towels.

To make the stuffing, melt the butter in a small frying pan over medium heat, add the spring onions and garlic and cook, stirring, until softened. Combine the breadcrumbs and pumpkin in a bowl. Add the spring onion mixture and season with salt and pepper. Spoon the stuffing into the chicken cavity. Close the cavity using poultry pins or by tying the legs together with string. Tuck the neck flap underneath.

Combine the oil and golden syrup or honey in a small saucepan and heat until warm, then brush all over the chicken. Sprinkle lightly with salt and pepper.

Put the chicken in the roasting tin and roast for 1¼–1½ hours, basting every 15 minutes with the pan juices. Cover with oiled foil if the chicken starts to over-brown. It is cooked when the juices run clear when a skewer is inserted into the thickest part of the thigh. Rest for 10 minutes before carving.

HINTS:
• Make your own gluten-free breadcrumbs by placing gluten-free bread slices in a food processor and blend until crumbs form—you'll need about 3 average slices of gluten-free bread without crusts.
• You can experiment with the stuffing. For example, you can replace the breadcrumbs with some cooked quinoa or buckwheat.
• Serve the chicken with roast potatoes and a variety of steamed vegetables.

FRESH TOMATO AND OLIVE PASTA

THIS PASTA SAUCE GOES EQUALLY WELL WITH GLUTEN-FREE OR REGULAR PASTA SO IT'S EASY TO PREPARE SEPARATE MEALS FOR THE GLUTEN-TOLERANT MEMBERS OF YOUR FAMILY. JUST REMEMBER TO USE A SEPARATE POT.

750 g (1 lb 10 oz) vine-ripened tomatoes, finely chopped
1 small red onion, finely chopped
2 garlic cloves, finely chopped
110 g (3½ oz/½ cup) chopped pitted green olives in brine
3 tbsp capers, rinsed, drained and chopped
1 tsp dried oregano
3 tbsp olive oil

1 tbsp white wine vinegar
500 g (1 lb 2 oz) gluten-free rigatoni
300 g (10½ oz) tin butter beans GF, drained and rinsed
1 handful oregano

PREP TIME: 15 MINUTES + 1 HOUR STANDING
COOKING TIME: 10 MINUTES
SERVES 4

Combine the tomatoes, onion, garlic, olives, capers and dried oregano in a bowl. Whisk together the oil and vinegar in a small bowl, then toss through the tomato mixture. Season with salt and pepper. Cover and set aside for at least 1 hour to allow the flavours to develop.

Meanwhile, cook the pasta in a large saucepan of boiling salted water for 10 minutes, or according to the packet instructions, until just tender. Drain and return to the saucepan. Toss the tomato mixture and butter beans through the hot pasta. Divide among four bowls, then garnish with the oregano leaves.

HINTS:
• You can use any type of gluten-free pasta shapes.
• If you prefer, omit the beans or replace them with soya beans, chickpeas or lentils, but remember to check the label for any gluten-containing additives.

nutrition per serve: Energy 2684 kJ (641 Cal); Fat 15.7 g; Saturated fat 2.4 g; Protein 10.7 g; Carbohydrate 110.4 g; Fibre 7.9 g; Cholesterol 0 mg

HAMBURGERS

YOU DON'T NEED TO GIVE UP FUN FOODS LIKE HAMBURGERS JUST BECAUSE YOU'RE ON A GLUTEN-FREE DIET. IN FACT, THE MEAT IN HAMBURGERS IS AN EXCELLENT SOURCE OF IRON, ZINC AND VITAMIN B12.

500 g (1 lb 2 oz) lean minced (ground) beef
4 spring onions (scallions), thinly sliced
3 tbsp snipped chives
1 garlic clove, crushed
1 egg
25 g (1 oz/1¼ cups) gluten-free puffed rice, finely crushed
canola or olive oil, for frying
12 slices of gluten-free bread

40 g (1½ oz) butter
½ head lettuce, shredded
chutney GF or tomato sauce GF (Basics)

PREP TIME: 30 MINUTES
COOKING TIME: 20 MINUTES
MAKES 6

Combine the beef, spring onions, chives, garlic, egg, puffed rice and 3 tablespoons water in a large bowl. Season with salt and pepper. Using your hands, knead the mixture until well combined. Divide the mixture into six portions. Roll into balls, then flatten into patties. Heat the oil in a large frying pan over medium heat, add the patties and cook for about 4–6 minutes on each side, or until cooked through and lightly browned.

Use a large biscuit (cookie) cutter to cut the bread into rounds. Otherwise, leave the slices square. Spread one side of each bread slice with butter and grill (broil), butter side up, for 1–2 minutes, or until crisp and golden brown.

Place a patty and lettuce between two slices of toasted bread. Serve topped with a dollop of chutney or tomato sauce.

HINTS:
• Use a gluten-free bread that toasts well and won't go soggy when you add the hamburger. If you try different brands of gluten-free bread on a regular basis, you can work out which ones toast better than others. Some will have a lighter texture than others. A stronger bread works best with a hamburger.
• These burgers are great for kids because they are fairly plain, perfect for fussy eaters. You can make them more interesting by adding other ingredients. For instance, hide a little grated carrot and zucchini in the beef patties to secretly get children to eat some more vegetables—add a little beaten egg to help bind the mixture. A slice of low-fat cheddar cheese in the burger is another good addition as it will provide extra calcium.

nutrition per serve: Energy 1728 kJ (413 Cal); Fat 13.3 g; Saturated fat 6.5 g; Protein 24.2 g; Carbohydrate 48.4 g; Fibre 1.5 g; Cholesterol 96 mg

GREEK-STYLE LAMB

400 g (14 oz) lean lamb fillets
1 tsp olive oil
1 large red onion, sliced
3 zucchini (courgettes), thinly sliced
200 g (7 oz) cherry tomatoes, halved
3 garlic cloves, crushed
60 g (2¼ oz/½ cup) pitted black olives in
  brine, drained and halved
2 tbsp lemon juice
2 tbsp oregano
100 g (3½ oz/⅔ cup) crumbled low-fat feta
  cheese
4 tbsp pine nuts, lightly toasted

PREP TIME: 20 MINUTES
COOKING TIME: 10 MINUTES
SERVES 4

Trim the lamb, then cut across the grain into thin strips. Heat a large frying pan until hot and lightly brush with oil. Add the lamb in small batches and cook each batch over high heat for 1–2 minutes, or until browned. Remove all the lamb from the pan.

Heat the oil in the pan, then add the onion and zucchini. Cook, stirring, over high heat for 2 minutes, or until just tender. Add the cherry tomatoes and garlic. Cook for 1–2 minutes, or until the tomatoes have just softened. Return the meat to the pan and stir over high heat until heated through.

Remove the pan from the heat. Add the olives, lemon juice and oregano and toss until well combined. Sprinkle with crumbled feta cheese and pine nuts before serving.

HINT:
• Serve with gluten-free bread rolls or corn tortillas and a mixed green salad.

THIS DISH IS SURE TO IMPRESS
YOUR FRIENDS AND FAMILY, BUT
YOU DON'T NEED TO SAVE IT FOR
SPECIAL OCCASIONS—IT MAKES A
GOOD WEEKDAY MEAL. YOU CAN
ALSO SERVE THIS DISH WITH RICE
INSTEAD OF GLUTEN-FREE BREAD,
IF YOU PREFER.

nutrition per serve   Energy 1892 kJ (451 Cal)
Fat 20 g
Saturated fat 5.5 g
Protein 34.6 g
Carbohydrate 31.1 g
Fibre 7.2 g
Cholesterol 78 mg

119

PORK AND CABBAGE NOODLE STIR-FRY

STIR-FRIES ARE A GREAT WAY TO MAKE HEALTHY MEALS WHEN YOU'RE SHORT OF TIME—JUST HAVE ALL THE INGREDIENTS READY BEFORE YOU BEGIN.

SAUCE
1½ tbsp fish sauce GF
4 tbsp tamari GF
1½ tbsp grated palm sugar or soft brown sugar

375 g (13 oz) thin rice stick noodles
2 tsp canola or olive oil
1 onion, finely chopped
2 garlic cloves, finely chopped
1–2 long red chillies, seeded and finely chopped

500 g (1 lb 2 oz) lean minced (ground) pork
1 large carrot, peeled and grated
1 zucchini (courgette), grated
225 g (8 oz/3 cups) thinly shredded cabbage
1 large handful coriander (cilantro) leaves

PREP TIME: 15 MINUTES
COOKING TIME: 10 MINUTES
SERVES 4

Combine the sauce ingredients in a small bowl, stirring to dissolve the sugar. Place the noodles in a large bowl and cover with boiling water. Set aside for 4 minutes, or until softened. Drain well. Use scissors to cut the noodles into shorter lengths.

Heat the oil in a wok. Add the onion, garlic, chilli and pork and stir-fry for 4 minutes, or until browned and cooked. Break up any lumps as you cook.

Stir in the carrot, zucchini and cabbage and continue to stir-fry for a further 2–3 minutes, or until the vegetables are just cooked. Stir through the noodles, then the sauce ingredients and coriander leaves.

HINTS:
• Always check the ingredient list on bottles of tamari and fish sauce as they can be hidden sources of gluten.
• If you prefer spicy food, leave the seeds in the chilli.

nutrition per serve: Energy 2309 kJ (552 Cal); Fat 12.5 g; Saturated fat 3.5 g; Protein 35.3 g; Carbohydrate 71.7 g; Fibre 5.9 g; Cholesterol 75 mg

FISH STEAKS WITH MUSHROOMS

THIS ASIAN-STYLE RECIPE WILL APPEAL TO FISH LOVERS AS IT CAN BE USED TO PREPARE SEVERAL DIFFERENT TYPES OF FISH (SNAPPER, SWORDFISH, COD, SALMON AND HALIBUT, TO NAME A FEW).

2 tbsp tamari GF

1 tbsp canola or olive oil

grated zest and juice of 1 lemon

2 tbsp Chinese rice wine or dry sherry

4 x 200 g (7 oz) snapper steaks

1 tsp sesame oil

150 g (5½ oz) fresh shiitake mushrooms, sliced

2 spring onions (scallions), sliced

PREP TIME: 15 MINUTES +
  4 HOURS MARINATING

COOKING TIME: 35 MINUTES

SERVES 4

Mix the tamari, oil, lemon zest and juice and rice wine or sherry together in a bowl. Put the fish steaks in a shallow, glass or ceramic ovenproof dish in which they fit snugly in a single layer. Pour the marinade over the fish and turn them once so both sides are coated. Cover and refrigerate for at least 4 hours, or overnight, turning the fish over in the marinade a couple of times.

Remove the fish from the fridge and let it return to room temperature. Preheat the oven to 180°C (350°F/Gas 4).

Heat the sesame oil in a frying pan over medium heat and, when hot, add the mushrooms. Cook and stir for 3–4 minutes, or until starting to soften. Add the spring onions, then stir and remove the pan from the heat.

Sprinkle the mushroom and onion mixture over the fish and bake, covered with a lid or foil, for 25–30 minutes, or until the fish is opaque and firm to the touch.

HINTS:
• Although tamari is usually wheat free, it is not always gluten free.
• Chinese rice wine (sometimes labelled Shaoxing) is available at Asian food stores. If you can't find it, use dry sherry instead.
• Serve with rice or gluten-free noodles and steamed green vegetables or salad.

nutrition per serve: Energy 1170 kJ (279 Cal); Fat 8.1 g; Saturated fat 1.8 g; Protein 42.2 g; Carbohydrate 6 g; Fibre 1.1 g; Cholesterol 122 mg

121

A SEAFOOD BUFFET IN ONE MEAL—
THIS DISH COMBINES A DELICIOUS
MIX OF SEAFOOD WITH A HERBED
RISOTTO FOR A FILLING, NUTRITIOUS
MEAL. IT'S A GOOD SOURCE OF
PROTEIN AND MINERALS INCLUDING
IRON, ZINC, IODINE AND SELENIUM.

nutrition per serve

Energy 2580 kJ (616 Cal)
Fat 5.8 g
Saturated fat 1.4 g
Protein 40.6 g
Carbohydrate 92.6 g
Fibre 1.3 g
Cholesterol 233 mg

SEAFOOD RISOTTO

12 black mussels
125 ml (4 fl oz/½ cup) dry white wine
1.5 litres (52 fl oz/6 cups) fish or chicken
   stock* (Basics)
1 small pinch of saffron threads
2 tsp olive oil
8 raw prawns (shrimp), peeled and
   deveined, tails intact
8 scallops, trimmed with coral intact
3 small squid tubes, cleaned and cut into
   rings

1 onion, finely chopped
2 garlic cloves, crushed
440 g (15½ oz/2 cups) arborio rice
2 tbsp chopped flat-leaf (Italian) parsley

PREP TIME: 25 MINUTES
COOKING TIME: 45 MINUTES
SERVES 4

Scrub the mussels with a stiff brush and remove the beards. Discard any broken mussels or any that don't close when tapped. Place the mussels in a heavy-based saucepan with the wine and cook, covered, over high heat, for 3–4 minutes, or until the mussels have just opened. Remove any that have not opened and discard. Strain and reserve the liquid and set the mussels aside.

Combine the mussel liquid, stock and saffron in a saucepan, then cover and keep at a low simmer. Heat 1 teaspoon of the oil in a non-stick frying pan over medium–high heat. Add the prawns and cook until they just turn pink. Remove to a plate, then cook the scallops and squid in batches for 1–2 minutes, or until lightly golden. Remove and set aside with the mussels and prawns.

Heat the remaining teaspoon of oil in a heavy-based saucepan, then add the onion and garlic. Reduce the heat to low and cook for 5–6 minutes, or until soft and translucent. Add the rice and stir until coated. Add 125 ml (4 fl oz/½ cup) of the hot stock, stirring constantly with a wooden spoon until absorbed. Continue adding 125 ml (4 fl oz/½ cup) of liquid at a time, stirring constantly, until all the liquid is absorbed. This should take about 25 minutes. Stir through the seafood and parsley. Season to taste and serve immediately.

HINTS:
• If you're using a commercial stock, make sure it doesn't contain gluten.
• Serve with a mixed leaf salad dressed with balsamic vinegar.

THAI CHICKEN SALAD

ENJOY THIS DELICIOUS, FRAGRANT SALAD WHEN THE WEATHER IS WARM. IT'S LIGHT AND REFRESHING SO IS THE PERFECT CHOICE. YOU CAN SPICE IT UP WITH RED CHILLI, IF YOU LIKE.

100 g (3½ oz) dried rice vermicelli

250 g (9 oz) minced (ground) chicken

200 g (7 oz) tin water chestnuts, drained and chopped

2 tbsp fish sauce GF

2 tbsp lime juice

1 lemon grass stem, white part only, finely chopped

3 spring onions (scallions), thinly sliced

3 tbsp chopped Thai basil

3 tbsp chopped mint

PREP TIME: 15 MINUTES +
10 MINUTES SOAKING

COOKING TIME: 5 MINUTES

SERVES 4

Put the dried rice vermicelli in a large bowl. Pour over enough boiling water to cover and soak for 10 minutes, or until tender. Drain and pat dry.

Put the chicken, water chestnuts, fish sauce, lime juice, lemon grass and 3 tablespoons water in a frying pan and stir over medium heat for 5 minutes, or until the chicken is cooked. Set aside to cool. Transfer to a bowl and add the spring onions, basil, mint and vermicelli. Toss well to combine. Serve immediately.

HINTS:
• Fish sauce can be a hidden source of gluten in Asian food so always check the label.
• Thai basil is distinguishable by its purple stems and flowers. If you can't find it, use normal basil instead.

nutrition per serve: Energy 798 kJ (191 Cal); Fat 5.2 g; Saturated fat 1.4 g; Protein 13.7 g; Carbohydrate 21 g; Fibre 1.8 g; Cholesterol 55 mg

SPICED LAMB WITH DAL AND YOGHURT

THIS DISH IS A REAL PLEASURE TO MAKE—THE SPICES WILL FILL YOUR
KITCHEN WITH DELICIOUS AROMAS THAT WILL STIMULATE YOUR APPETITE.

3 tsp cumin seeds

1 tbsp coriander seeds

1 tsp garam masala

2 x 250 g (9 oz) lean lamb loin fillets

400 g (14 oz/2 cups) long-grain white rice

low-fat plain yoghurt GF, to serve

DAL

200 g (7 oz/¾ cup heaped) red lentils

¼ tsp ground turmeric

750 ml (26 fl oz/3 cups) chicken stock GF
   (Basics)

2 tsp brown mustard seeds

2 tsp ground cumin

1 onion, finely chopped

3 garlic cloves, crushed

½ tsp chilli flakes

3 tbsp chopped coriander (cilantro) leaves

PREP TIME: 20 MINUTES +
   2 HOURS MARINATING
COOKING TIME: 1 HOUR
SERVES 4

Put the cumin and coriander seeds and garam masala in a small, dry frying pan and toast for 1 minute, or until fragrant. Put in a spice grinder, or use a mortar and pestle, and grind until coarse. Season, then rub onto the lamb. Cover and refrigerate for 2 hours.

Bring 1 litre (35 fl oz/4 cups) water to the boil in a large saucepan. Stir in the rice. Cover the pan, reduce the heat and simmer for 20 minutes. Uncover, stir and stand for 5 minutes.

To make the dal, put the lentils and turmeric in a saucepan, cover with the stock and bring to the boil over high heat. Reduce the heat to low and simmer for 20 minutes, stirring occasionally, or until the lentils are tender.

Spray a non-stick saucepan with canola or olive oil, then heat over high heat. Add the mustard seeds and cumin and cook for 1 minute, or until the mustard seeds begin to pop. Add the onion and cook for 2–3 minutes, or until softened. Add the garlic and chilli and cook for 30 seconds. Add the lentil mixture and coriander, reduce the heat to low and cook for 5 minutes, stirring, or until reduced and thickened. Keep warm.

Lightly spray a chargrill plate with oil and heat over high heat. Add the lamb and cook for 4–5 minutes on each side. Cover and stand for 5 minutes. Cut into 1 cm (½ in) slices on the diagonal. Divide the rice and dal onto four plates and top with the lamb. Serve with yoghurt.

nutrition per serve: Energy 3030 kJ (724 Cal); Fat 10.9 g; Saturated fat 2.8 g; Protein 48.8 g; Carbohydrate 103.7 g; Fibre 9.8 g; Cholesterol 85 mg

CHICKEN AND LEEK PIE

350 g (12 oz) boneless, skinless chicken
  breast
30 g (1 oz) butter
1 leek, washed and thinly sliced
1 celery stalk, thinly sliced
4 slices of low-fat bacon GF, thinly sliced
2 tsp pure maize cornflour (cornstarch) GF
185 ml (6 fl oz/¾ cup) low-fat milk
1 egg yolk
1 small handful parsley, chopped

125 g (4½ oz/1 cup firmly packed) grated
  low-fat cheddar cheese GF
1 quantity gluten-free shortcrust pastry
  (Basics)

PREP TIME: 30 MINUTES +
  20 MINUTES STANDING
COOKING TIME: 55 MINUTES
SERVES 4

To make the filling, put the chicken in a saucepan and cover with cold water. Slowly bring to the boil, then simmer for 2 minutes. Turn off the heat, cover and set aside 20 minutes.

Heat the butter in a medium frying pan. Add the leek, celery and bacon. Cook, stirring occasionally for 5 minutes over low heat until the leek is soft. In a small bowl combine the cornflour with a little of the milk. Mix until smooth. Add the remaining milk and egg yolk. Pour over the leek mixture. Stir over a low heat for 2–3 minutes until thickened. Season with salt and pepper.

Shred the chicken with a fork, then stir it into the leek mixture. Transfer to a plate to cool completely, then stir in the parsley. Preheat the oven to 200°C (400°F/Gas 6).

Lightly grease a 23 cm (9 in) fluted flan tin, then line it with the prepared pastry. Trim to fit the tin. The pastry is soft and malleable so just fill any tears and cracks if necessary. Reserve the leftover dough.

Place the tin on a baking tray. Cover the pastry with a sheet of baking paper and half fill with baking beads or rice. Bake for 10 minutes. Remove the beads and paper and bake for a further 10–15 minutes, or until lightly browned. Fill any cracks with small amounts of reserved pastry. Bake for a further 2 minutes to set. Remove from the oven and cool completely. Reduce the oven temperature to 180°C (350°F/Gas 4).

Fill the cooled pastry with the cooled filling. Scatter the cheese over the top. Bake for 20 minutes until cooked and the pastry is golden brown.

HINT:
• Serve with a mixed salad or steamed vegetables.

PIES ARE A GREAT COMFORT
FOOD, PARTICULARLY IN WINTER.
THIS RECIPE WILL HELP
CONVINCE NEWLY DIAGNOSED
COELIACS THAT A GLUTEN-FREE
DIET DOESN'T HAVE TO BE A
BLAND, BORING AFFAIR.

nutrition per serve Energy 2717 kJ (649 Cal)

Fat 31.8 g

Saturated fat 19.2 g

Protein 42.2 g

Carbohydrate 48.4 g

Fibre 1.8 g

Cholesterol 249 mg

BEEF AND NOODLE SALAD

SPICE UP YOUR WEEKLY MENU WITH THIS ASIAN-STYLE SALAD, WHICH IS QUICK AND EASY TO MAKE. THE MIXTURE OF HERBS ADDS LOTS OF FLAVOUR AND AROMA AS WELL AS FOLATE AND ANTIOXIDANTS.

DRESSING

2 tbsp finely chopped lemon grass, white part only

1 small red chilli

3 tbsp tamari GF

3 tbsp lime juice

1 tbsp fish sauce GF

1 tbsp grated palm sugar or soft brown sugar

1 tsp grated fresh ginger

500 g (1 lb 2 oz) lean sirloin steak

200 g (7 oz) cellophane (bean thread) noodles

1 Lebanese (short) cucumber

1 small red onion

4 ripe Roma (plum) tomatoes

1 tbsp thinly shredded fresh ginger

90 g (3¼ oz/1 cup) bean sprouts, trimmed

1 handful mint, torn

1 handful basil, torn

1 handful coriander (cilantro) leaves

PREP TIME: 15 MINUTES +
   15 MINUTES MARINATING

COOKING TIME: 10 MINUTES

SERVES 4

Bruise the lemon grass using a mortar and pestle or a heavy object such as a rolling pin. Seed and finely chop the chilli. Combine the dressing ingredients using a mortar and pestle or in a bowl and stir to dissolve the sugar. Put 1 tablespoon of the dressing in a shallow non-metallic dish with the meat. Coat the meat with the dressing and marinate for at least 15 minutes. Set aside the remaining dressing.

Spray a non-stick frying pan or chargrill pan with oil. Heat the oil until very hot. Add the steak and cook for 2–3 minutes on each side, or until cooked as desired. Remove and set aside for 5 minutes, then slice thinly.

Place the noodles in a large bowl and cover with boiling water. Set aside for 4 minutes, drain well and refresh under cold water. Use scissors to cut into short lengths.

Cut the cucumber in half lengthways, then thinly slice on the diagonal. Cut the onion into thin wedges. Cut the tomatoes into quarters. Put into a large bowl with the rest of the ingredients. Toss together gently with the remaining dressing so everything is covered. Serve immediately.

nutrition per serve: Energy 1736 kJ (415 Cal); Fat 8.9 g; Saturated fat 3.5 g; Protein 29.7 g; Carbohydrate 51.7 g; Fibre 3 g; Cholesterol 72 mg

WARM PRAWN AND SCALLOP STIR-FRY

THIS DISH IS QUITE SIMPLE TO MAKE—JUST HAVE ALL OF THE INGREDIENTS
MEASURED AND READY TO GO BEFORE YOU FIRE THE WOK UP.

400 g (14 oz/2 cups) basmati rice, rinsed
and drained

2 tsp five-spice

1–2 small red chillies, seeded and finely
chopped

2–3 garlic cloves, crushed

2 tsp sesame oil

500 g (1 lb 2 oz) raw prawns (shrimp),
peeled and deveined, tails intact

300 g (10½ oz) scallops, trimmed, with
coral intact

200 g (7 oz) asparagus, trimmed and cut
into short lengths

150 g (5½ oz) snow peas (mangetout),
trimmed

125 g (4½ oz/2¾ cups) roughly chopped
rocket (arugula)

2 tbsp tamari GF

2 tbsp lemon juice

1 tbsp mirin

2 tsp honey

6 spring onions (scallions), sliced

1 tbsp chopped coriander (cilantro) leaves

1 tbsp sesame seeds, toasted

PREP TIME: 30 MINUTES +
    10 MINUTES MARINATING
COOKING TIME: 35 MINUTES
SERVES 4

Put the rice and 1 litre (35 fl oz/4 cups) water in a saucepan and bring to the boil over
medium heat. Reduce the heat to low, cover with a lid and cook for 20 minutes, or until
the rice is tender. Remove from the heat and leave to stand, covered, for 5 minutes.

Meanwhile, combine the five-spice, chilli, garlic and sesame oil in a large non-metallic
bowl. Add the prawns and scallops and toss to coat. Cover with plastic wrap and
refrigerate for at least 10 minutes.

Blanch the asparagus and snow peas. Drain and plunge into a bowl of iced water, then
drain again. Arrange on four plates with the rocket. Combine the tamari, lemon juice, mirin
and honey in a small bowl.

Heat a wok over high heat, add the seafood and spring onions in batches and cook for
3–4 minutes, or until cooked through, reheating the wok between batches. Remove from
the wok and set aside. Add the tamari–lemon sauce and coriander to the wok, then bring
to the boil. Cook over high heat for 1–2 minutes. Return the seafood to the wok and toss
well. Divide among the plates and sprinkle with the sesame seeds. Serve with the rice.

nutrition per serve: Energy 2291 kJ (545 Cal); Fat 5.8 g; Saturated fat 0.8 g; Protein 33.2 g;
Carbohydrate 88.7 g; Fibre 4.7 g; Cholesterol 118 mg

DESSERTS

FOR A COMFORTING WINTER
DESSERT, YOU CAN'T GO PAST
APPLE PIE. YOU MAY NEED TO
PRACTISE MAKING THIS PIE A FEW
TIMES BECAUSE GLUTEN-FREE
PASTRY CAN BE A BIT MORE
TRICKY TO WORK WITH THAN
PASTRY BASED ON WHEAT FLOUR.

nutrition per serve (8) Energy 1081 kJ (258 Cal)
Fat 10.1 g
Saturated fat 6.3 g
Protein 1.8 g
Carbohydrate 39.8 g
Fibre 1.7 g
Cholesterol 52 mg

APPLE AND BERRY PIE

400 g (14 oz) tin pie (bakers) apples GF
3 tbsp caster (superfine) sugar
1 tsp grated lemon zest
1 tbsp polenta
1 quantity gluten-free sweet shortcrust
   pastry (Basics)
165 g (5¾ oz/1½ cups) mixed fresh
   or frozen berries
raw (demerara) sugar, to sprinkle

PREP TIME: 30 MINUTES + CHILLING
COOKING TIME: 45 MINUTES
SERVES 6–8

Preheat the oven to 200°C (400°F/Gas 6). Lightly grease a pie dish or pie tin that is 18 cm (7 in) across the base. Put the apples, caster sugar, lemon zest and polenta in a bowl and stir to combine.

Roll the pastry between two sheets of baking paper to a rough 30 cm (12 in) circle. Carefully turn the pastry into the prepared dish with the pastry overlapping the edge of the dish.

Stir the berries through the apple mixture, then add the apple and berry mixture to the centre of the pastry. Fold over the overlapping edges leaving the fruit in the centre exposed. Sprinkle the pastry with raw sugar.

Put the dish on a baking tray. Bake for 35-45 minutes, or until the pastry is crisp and lightly browned. Cover with foil if browning too much. Serve hot or warm.

HINTS:
• If you can't find a gluten-free version of canned pie apple, then use home-made stewed apples instead.
• If you have diabetes, you can replace the caster sugar with sucralose.
• Low-fat gluten-free vanilla ice cream or custard is delicious with this pie.

SPICED CREAMED RICE WITH APRICOTS

THIS CREAMY DESSERT IS BOTH DELICIOUS AND VERSATILE. YOU CAN ADD
SOME CHOPPED BLANCHED ALMONDS TO THE MIXTURE IF YOU LIKE.

24 dried apricot halves
750 ml (26 fl oz/3 cups) skim milk
110 g (3¾ oz/½ cup) arborio rice
1 vanilla bean, split lengthways
¼ tsp ground nutmeg
pinch of ground cardamom
2 tsp caster (superfine) sugar
165 g (5¾ oz/¾ cup) sugar

2 cinnamon sticks
2 tsp grated orange zest
3 tbsp orange juice

PREP TIME: 10 MINUTES +
    30 MINUTES SOAKING
COOKING TIME: 50 MINUTES
SERVES 4–6

Put the apricots in a heatproof bowl, cover with boiling water and leave to soak for
30 minutes, or until the apricots are plump.

Pour the milk into a saucepan, add the rice, vanilla bean, nutmeg and cardamom and bring
to the boil. Reduce the heat and simmer gently, stirring frequently, for 25 minutes, or until
the rice is soft and creamy and has absorbed most of the milk. Remove from the heat.

Remove the vanilla bean, scrape out the seeds with the tip of a knife and mix them into
the rice. Stir in the caster sugar.

Meanwhile, to make the sugar syrup, put the sugar, cinnamon sticks, orange zest and juice
in a saucepan with 625 ml (21½ fl oz/2½ cups) water. Bring to the boil, then reduce the heat
and simmer for 10 minutes. Drain the apricots and add to the pan. Return to the boil, then
reduce the heat to low and simmer for 5 minutes, or until soft. Remove the apricots with a
slotted spoon. Return the sauce to the boil, then boil until reduced by half. Remove from the
heat, cool a little and pour over the apricots. Serve the apricots with the creamed rice.

HINTS:
• If you're lactose intolerant, you can use rice milk or light gluten-free soy milk instead of
  the skim milk.
• If you have diabetes, you can lower the GI of this dish by replacing the arborio rice
  (medium GI) with a lower GI rice, such as koshikari or doongara. You can also replace the
  sugar with sucralose. This will reduce the kilojoule and carbohydrate content and help
  reduce the GI.

nutrition per serve (6): Energy 1079 kJ (257 Cal); Fat 0.3 g; Saturated fat 0.2 g; Protein 6.6 g;
Carbohydrate 57.9 g; Fibre 1.6 g; Cholesterol 4 mg

APPLE SNOW

THIS LIGHT REFRESHING DESSERT IS LOW GI AND LOW IN FAT AND
KILOJOULES. IT'S A GREAT CHOICE FOR PEOPLE WITH DIABETES OR
LACTOSE INTOLERANCE AS WELL AS THOSE WATCHING THEIR WEIGHT.

4 green apples, peeled, cored and chopped
1 tsp sugar
½ tsp ground cinnamon
2 tsp powdered gelatine
3 egg whites

PREP TIME: 10 MINUTES +
30 MINUTES REFRIGERATION
COOKING TIME: 10 MINUTES
SERVES 4

Put the chopped apples, sugar, cinnamon and 3 tablespoons water in a saucepan. Simmer, covered, for 8 minutes, or until tender. Mash until puréed.

Sprinkle the gelatine over 1 tablespoon of water in a small heatproof bowl and leave to go spongy. Put the bowl in a saucepan of just boiled water, off the heat (the water should come halfway up the bowl). Stir to dissolve. Stir into the hot purée.

Beat the egg whites until stiff peaks form, then fold into the hot purée—the heat should slightly cook the whites. Spoon the mixture into glass bowls or parfait glasses, then refrigerate for at least 30 minutes before serving.

HINT:
• This dessert has a low GI with or without sugar. However, if you have diabetes and prefer to use sucralose instead of sugar, substitute the sugar with ½ teaspoon sucralose. This will slightly lower the carbohydrate and kilojoule content and will reduce your blood-sugar response.

nutrition per serve: Energy 382 kJ (91 Cal); Fat 0.2 g; Saturated fat 0 g; Protein 4.5 g; Carbohydrate 18.8 g; Fibre 3 g; Cholesterol 0 mg

STRAWBERRY AND RASPBERRY PARFAIT

85 g (3 oz) packet diet strawberry-flavoured jelly (gelatin dessert) crystals

250 g (9 oz/1²/₃ cups) strawberries, hulled

500 g (1 lb 2 oz) low-fat vanilla ice cream
GF

125 g (4½ oz/1 cup) raspberries

PREP TIME: 10 MINUTES + 1 HOUR SETTING

COOKING TIME: NIL

SERVES 6

Put the jelly crystals in a heatproof bowl and pour over 250 ml (9 fl oz/1 cup) boiling water. Stir to dissolve the crystals, then add 250 ml (9 fl oz/1 cup) cold water. Put the bowl in the refrigerator for at least 1 hour, or until set.

Process the strawberries in a food processor for 15 seconds until blended to a pulp.

Layer the jelly, strawberry purée and ice cream into six parfait glasses. Top with raspberries, then serve immediately.

HINTS:
• Use thawed frozen raspberries if fresh are not available.
• This dessert has a low GI and is therefore suitable for people with diabetes.
• If you are lactose intolerant, you can use a lactose-free, gluten-free vanilla dessert, such as a soy 'ice cream' (available in the ice-cream section of supermarkets).

BOTH KIDS AND ADULTS WILL
LOVE THIS FUN DESSERT, WHICH
IS REALLY EASY TO MAKE. THE
BERRIES ADD A BURST OF
COLOUR, FLAVOUR, FIBRE
AND ANTIOXIDANTS.

nutrition per serve

Energy 701 kJ (167 Cal)
Fat 2.7 g
Saturated fat 1.7 g
Protein 18.1 g
Carbohydrate 18 g
Fibre 1.8 g
Cholesterol 8 mg

137

PEACHES WITH RICOTTA CREAM

DESSERT DOESN'T HAVE TO BE A GUILT-RIDDEN INDULGENCE: IT CAN BE AN OPPORTUNITY TO ADD SOME MORE NUTRITIOUS FOODS TO YOUR DIET AND REACH YOUR DAILY QUOTA OF FRESH FRUIT.

4 large peaches, unpeeled
500 ml (17 fl oz/2 cups) unsweetened
    apple juice
1 tbsp caster (superfine) sugar
2 tsp lemon juice
3 tbsp flaked almonds, lightly toasted

1 tsp natural vanilla extract
1 tsp grated lemon zest

PREP TIME: 20 MINUTES
COOKING TIME: 10 MINUTES
SERVES 4

RICOTTA CREAM
200 g (7 oz) low-fat ricotta cheese
1 tsp caster (superfine) sugar

Cut the peaches in half and remove the stone. Heat the apple juice in a saucepan over medium heat, then add the sugar and lemon juice and stir until dissolved. Add the peach halves and poach, covered, over low heat for 5–8 minutes, or until just tender when pierced with a knife. Remove with a slotted spoon and peel away the skins. Cool. Reserve the poaching juice.

To make the ricotta cream, put the ricotta, sugar, vanilla and lemon zest in a bowl and beat with electric beaters until smooth. Cover with plastic wrap, then refrigerate to firm.

Serve the peach halves with a little of the reserved juice, then spoon over the ricotta cream and sprinkle with the almonds.

HINTS:
• Use nectarines instead of the peaches, if you prefer.
• If fresh peaches are out of season, use an 825 g (1 lb 14 oz) can peach halves in natural juice, drained but reserving a little of the juice for serving.
• This is a low-GI dessert but people with diabetes can use a sweetener like sucralose instead of the sugar to reduce the GI and kilojoule content even further.

nutrition per serve: Energy 934 kJ (223 Cal); Fat 7.7 g; Saturated fat 3 g; Protein 8.3 g; Carbohydrate 29.2 g; Fibre 3.5 g; Cholesterol 21 mg

PASSIONFRUIT SORBET

SORBET IS A LIGHT REFRESHING DESSERT THAT'S THE PERFECT WAY TO END A MEAL. BEING LOWER IN FAT AND KILOJOULES THAN ICE CREAM IT'S A MUCH HEALTHIER CHOICE, SO YOU CAN INDULGE WITHOUT GUILT.

400 g (14 oz) tin peach slices in
    natural juice
400 g (14 oz) tin pear halves in
    natural juice
3 tbsp caster (superfine) sugar
4 tbsp fresh passionfruit pulp
1 tbsp lemon juice
2 egg whites
fresh fruit, to serve

PREP TIME: 15 MINUTES + FREEZING
COOKING TIME: NIL
SERVES 6

Drain the tinned fruit and reserve the juice. Put the reserved juice and sugar in a small saucepan. Stir over low heat for 2 minutes until the sugar has dissolved. Cool.

Strain the passionfruit pulp into a small bowl, reserving the seeds. Put the strained passionfruit juice, the drained tinned fruit, the cooled fruit juice and lemon juice in a food processor. Blend until smooth. Stir in the reserved passionfruit seeds.

Pour into a shallow 27 x 17 cm (10¾ x 6½ in) tin and freeze for 3 hours, stirring occasionally, until the mixture is icy. Use a fork to roughly mash the mixture. Put in a bowl and beat with electric beaters until smooth and creamy looking.

Beat the egg whites until firm peaks form, then fold into the creamed fruit mixture until just combined. Do not over-mix. Spoon into a 1.5 litre (52 fl oz/6 cup) loaf (bar) tin. Cover with plastic wrap and freeze until firm.

To serve, put the tin in the refrigerator for about 15 minutes to allow the sorbet to soften a little. Use an ice-cream scoop and serve 2–3 scoops of sorbet per person. Serve with fruit.

HINTS:
• If you have diabetes, you can replace the sugar with an equal amount of sucralose, which will reduce the GI and kilojoule content of the dessert. Choose low-GI fruit such as passionfruit, berries or stone fruit.
• You will need 3–4 large passionfruit to yield 4 tablespoons of pulp.

nutrition per serve: Energy 320 kJ (76 Cal); Fat 0.05 g; Saturated fat 0 g; Protein 2.4 g; Carbohydrate 16.3 g; Fibre 4 g; Cholesterol 0 mg

WARMING, COMFORTING
PUDDINGS OFTEN TOP THE LIST
OF FAVOURITE WINTERTIME
DESSERTS AND THIS ONE IS
NO EXCEPTION.

nutrition per serve   Energy 1708 kJ (408 Cal)
Fat 11.1 g
Saturated fat 6.5 g
Protein 4.8 g
Carbohydrate 72.8 g
Fibre 1.9 g
Cholesterol 61 mg

BUTTERSCOTCH PUDDING

190 g (6¾ oz/1¼ cups) gluten-free
   self-raising flour
1 tsp gluten-free baking powder
80 g (2¾ oz/⅓ cup firmly packed) soft
   brown sugar
170 ml (5½ fl oz/⅔ cup) milk
60 g (2¼ oz) unsalted butter, melted,
   cooled
1 egg

1 tbsp golden syrup or pure maple syrup
165 g (5¾ oz/¾ cup firmly packed) soft
   brown sugar, extra
2 tbsp golden syrup or pure maple syrup,
   extra

PREP TIME: 20 MINUTES

COOKING TIME: 45 MINUTES

SERVES 4–6

Preheat the oven to 170°C (325°F/Gas 3). Lightly grease a 1.25 litre (44 fl oz/5 cup) ovenproof dish.

Sift the flour and baking powder into a large bowl. Stir in the sugar, then make a well in the centre. In a separate bowl, whisk the milk, butter, egg and golden syrup or maple syrup together. Pour into the well in the dry ingredients and whisk until a smooth batter forms. Pour into the prepared dish. Place the dish on a baking tray.

Sprinkle the extra brown sugar over the batter. Combine the extra golden syrup or maple syrup and 420 ml (14½ fl oz/1⅔ cups) boiling water and carefully pour over the batter. Bake the pudding for 35–45 minutes, or until a skewer inserted halfway into the pudding comes out clean.

Set the pudding aside for 5–10 minutes to allow the sauce to thicken slightly before serving.

HINT:
• To make this free of dairy and egg, replace the milk with gluten-free rice drink, the butter with dairy-free margarine and the egg with egg replacer.

CHOCOLATE SELF-SAUCING PUDDING

THIS RECIPE IS A GLUTEN-FREE VERSION OF A FAMILY FAVOURITE AND IT MAKES THE PERFECT FINISHING TOUCH TO END A SPECIAL MEAL.

150 g (5½ oz/1¼ cups) soy-containing, gluten-free self-raising flour

1 tsp gluten-free baking powder

80 g (2¾ oz/⅓ cup firmly packed) soft brown sugar

125 ml (4 fl oz/½ cup) milk

2 tbsp pure unsweetened cocoa powder GF

60 g (2¼ oz) unsalted butter, melted, cooled

1 egg, lightly beaten

165 g (5¾ oz/¾ cup firmly packed) soft brown sugar, extra

2 tbsp pure unsweetened cocoa powder GF, extra

PREP TIME: 20 MINUTES

COOKING TIME: 45 MINUTES

SERVES 4–6

Preheat the oven to 170°C (325°F/Gas 3). Lightly grease a 1.25 litre (44 fl oz/5 cup) capacity ovenproof dish.

Sift the flour and baking powder into a large bowl and add the sugar; make a well in the centre. In a separate bowl, whisk the milk and cocoa powder together until smooth. Set aside to cool. Add the butter and egg to the cocoa mixture and whisk to combine. Pour into the well in the flour mixture and whisk until a smooth, thick batter forms. Pour into the prepared dish. Place the dish on a baking tray.

Sprinkle the extra brown sugar over the batter. Whisk 375 ml (13 fl oz/1½ cups) boiling water and the extra cocoa powder together until smooth. Carefully pour over the batter. Bake for 35–45 minutes, or until a skewer inserted halfway into the pudding comes out clean. Serve immediately.

HINTS:
• This recipe requires a gluten-free flour mixture that contains soya flour so check the ingredient list on the packet of flour. Flour with soy content behaves more like gluten flour and is necessary in some recipes.
• If you're lactose intolerant, replace the milk with 160 ml (5¼ fl oz/⅔ cup) rice drink or gluten-free soy milk and use dairy-free margarine.
• If you prefer, you can substitute the cocoa powder with carob powder to make a carob self-saucing pudding.

nutrition per serve (6): Energy 1571 kJ (375 Cal); Fat 10.5 g; Saturated fat 2.8 g; Protein 5.7 g; Carbohydrate 64.4 g; Fibre 2.1 g; Cholesterol 35 mg

APPLE SAGO PUDDING

SAGO IS DELICIOUS AND ADDS ANOTHER GLUTEN-FREE OPTION TO YOUR DIET. KIDS AND ADULTS WILL BOTH ENJOY THIS SWEET PUDDING, WHICH IS LIKE A MORE EXOTIC VERSION OF RICE PUDDING.

4 tbsp caster (superfine) sugar

100 g (3½ oz/½ cup) sago

600 ml (21 fl oz) milk

4 tbsp sultanas (golden raisins)

1 tsp natural vanilla extract

pinch of ground nutmeg

¼ tsp ground cinnamon

2 eggs, lightly beaten

3 small ripe apples (about 250 g/9 oz), peeled, cored and very thinly sliced

1 tbsp soft brown sugar

PREP TIME: 15 MINUTES

COOKING TIME: 50 MINUTES

SERVES 4

Preheat the oven to 180°C (350°F/Gas 4). Grease a 1.5 litre (52 fl oz/6 cup) ceramic soufflé dish. Place the sugar, sago, milk and sultanas in a saucepan. Heat the mixture, stirring often. Bring to the boil, then reduce the heat and simmer for 5 minutes.

Stir in the vanilla extract, nutmeg, cinnamon, egg and the apple slices, then pour the mixture into the prepared dish. Sprinkle with the brown sugar and bake for 45 minutes, or until set and golden brown.

HINT:
• Sago is similar to tapioca and is a dried starchy granule extracted from the pith of a type of palm tree. Cooks in the South Pacific frequently use sago for baking, thickening soups and making puddings and other desserts. It's a high-carbohydrate food, but its GI value has not yet been measured.

nutrition per serve: Energy 1621 kJ (387 Cal); Fat 8.7 g; Saturated fat 4.7 g; Protein 8.9 g; Carbohydrate 68.5 g; Fibre 2.3 g; Cholesterol 114 mg

BAKED RAISIN APPLES

4 cooking apples
80 g (2¾ oz/⅓ cup firmly packed) soft brown sugar
1½ tbsp chopped raisins
½ tsp ground cinnamon (optional)
20 g (¾ oz) unsalted butter
low-fat plain yoghurt or ricotta cream (page 138), to serve

PREP TIME: 10 MINUTES
COOKING TIME: 35 MINUTES
SERVES 4

Preheat the oven to 220°C (425°F/Gas 7). Use an apple corer to remove the core of the apples, then score the skin around the middle.

Combine the sugar, raisins and cinnamon in a bowl. Place each apple on a piece of heavy-duty foil and stuff it with the filling. Spread a little butter over the top of each apple, then wrap the foil securely around the apples. Bake for about 35 minutes, or until cooked. Serve with yoghurt or ricotta cream.

HINTS:
• Use apples of a similar size so they all cook evenly. The apples can also be baked in a covered barbecue.
• If you choose a flavoured yoghurt over plain, check the ingredient list to ensure it doesn't contain any gluten.
• If you prefer, serve the apples with gluten-free ice cream.

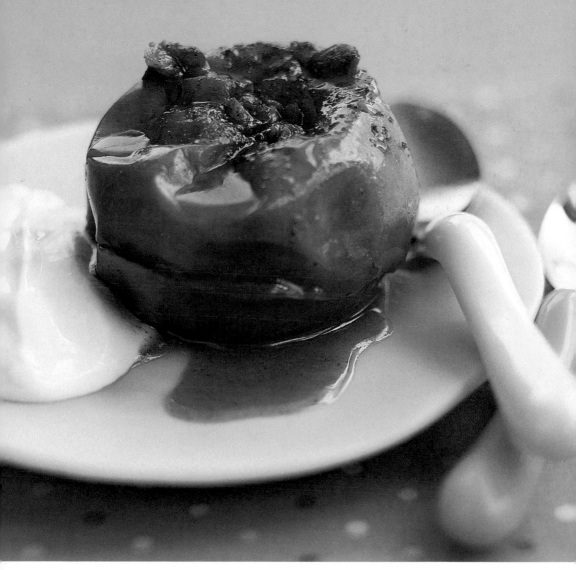

A SIMPLY DELICIOUS DESSERT
THAT PROVIDES A SWEET DOSE
OF FIBRE. THE COOKED APPLE
SKIN MAY NEED TO BE REMOVED
BEFORE BEING SERVED TO VERY
YOUNG CHILDREN.

nutrition per serve   Energy 859 kJ (205 Cal)
Fat 4.4 g
Saturated fat 2.7 g
Protein 0.7 g
Carbohydrate 40.8 g
Fibre 3.5 g
Cholesterol 13 mg

CREPES WITH COFFEE SAUCE

YOU CAN TEAM THESE CREPES WITH A NUMBER OF DIFFERENT TOPPINGS, SUCH AS PURE FRUIT JAM, LEMON JUICE AND SUGAR, OR EVEN GLUTEN-FREE CHOCOLATE SPREAD.

COFFEE SAUCE
2 tbsp golden syrup or pure maple syrup
3 tsp instant coffee powder
2 tbsp pure maize cornflour (cornstarch) GF
235 g (8½ oz/1 cup firmly packed) soft
brown sugar

CREPES
190 g (6¾ oz/1¼ cups) gluten-free plain
(all-purpose) flour
2 tsp gluten-free baking powder
1 egg
2 tbsp canola oil

PREP TIME: 35 MINUTES
COOKING TIME: 25 MINUTES
MAKES 10

To make the coffee sauce, combine the syrup, coffee powder, cornflour and sugar in a frying pan. Add 250 ml (9 fl oz/1 cup) water and blend. Put the pan over medium heat. Stir constantly until the mixture boils and thickens. Reduce the heat and simmer for 2–3 minutes. Set aside.

To make the crepes, sift the flour and baking powder into a bowl. Gradually add the combined egg, 1 tablespoon of the oil and 310 ml (10¾ fl oz/1¼ cups) water, stirring well until the batter is smooth and the consistency of thin cream, adding more water if needed. Strain into a vessel with a pouring lip.

Lightly brush a 20 cm (8 in) frying pan with a little of the remaining oil and heat over medium heat. Pour in just enough crepe batter to thinly cover the bottom of the pan. When the top of the crepe starts to set, turn it over with a spatula. After browning the second side, transfer to a plate. Repeat with the remaining crepe batter, greasing the pan between each. Fold each crepe in four to form a triangle.

Reheat the sauce in a frying pan over low heat. Put the crepes in the pan and heat gently until warmed through. Place the crepes on two serving plates and spoon any extra warm sauce over the top.

HINT:
• If you have diabetes, use pure maple syrup (low GI) instead of golden syrup (medium GI).

nutrition per crepe with sauce: Energy 933 kJ (223 Cal); Fat 4.3 g; Saturated fat 0.4 g; Protein 1.1 g; Carbohydrate 45.7 g; Fibre 0.4 g; Cholesterol 19 mg

POACHED PEARS IN VANILLA–LEMON SYRUP

THESE PEARS ARE DELICIOUS EITHER WARM OR COLD AND MAKE A STYLISH, YET HEALTHY, DESSERT—GOOD ENOUGH TO SERVE AT DINNER PARTIES.

170 g (6 oz/¾ cup) caster (superfine) sugar
1 vanilla bean, split lengthways and scraped
1 strip lemon zest
1½ tsp lemon grass tea leaves
4 large firm pears, peeled with stems intact
4 tbsp low-fat plain yoghurt

PREP TIME: 15 MINUTES
COOKING TIME: 50 MINUTES
SERVES 4

Put the sugar, vanilla bean and lemon zest in a large saucepan with 500 ml (17 fl oz/ 2 cups) water. Put the lemon grass in a tea-infuser ball or small muslin (cheesecloth) bag, and add to the saucepan. Heat over low heat, stirring occasionally, until the sugar melts.

Bring to the boil, then reduce to a simmer and add the pears, laying them on their sides. Cover and simmer, turning occasionally, for 30 minutes, or until the pears are tender when pierced with a skewer.

Remove the pears with a slotted spoon and set aside to cool. Meanwhile, increase the heat to high and simmer the syrup for 8–10 minutes, or until reduced by half and thickened slightly. Remove the vanilla bean, lemon zest and lemon grass tea. Serve the pears drizzled with the syrup and a dollop of the yoghurt on the side.

HINTS:
- If you have diabetes, you can make this a low-GI dessert by using sucralose instead of sugar. This will also reduce the kilojoule content.
- If you place the lemon grass tea in a tea-infuser ball or muslin bag, it can readily be removed, as it is too fine to be strained from the syrup.
- You can use a flavoured yoghurt instead of plain, if you prefer; remember to check the label because many flavoured yoghurts contain gluten.

nutrition per serve: Energy 1227 kJ (293 Cal); Fat 0.2 g; Saturated fat 0.02 g; Protein 1.8 g; Carbohydrate 72 g; Fibre 3.7 g; Cholesterol 1 mg

THIS REFRESHING BLEND OF
TROPICAL FRUIT IS A GOOD
SOURCE OF FIBRE, VITAMIN C,
POTASSIUM AND OTHER
ANTIOXIDANTS AND MAKES A
HEALTHY, GUILT-FREE DESSERT.

nutrition per serve

Energy 936 kJ (224 Cal)
Fat 0.8 g
Saturated fat 0.01 g
Protein 3.4 g
Carbohydrate 47.8 g
Fibre 7.2 g
Cholesterol 0 g

LEMON GRASS AND GINGER FRUIT SALAD

3 tbsp caster (superfine) sugar
2 x 2 cm (¾ x ¾ in) piece of fresh ginger, thinly sliced
1 lemon grass stem, bruised and halved
pulp from 1 large passionfruit
1 Fiji red pawpaw
½ honeydew melon
1 large mango

1 small pineapple
12 lychees
1 large handful mint, shredded, to serve

PREP TIME: 20 MINUTES
COOKING TIME: 10 MINUTES
SERVES 4

Place the sugar, ginger and lemon grass in a small saucepan, add 125 ml (4 fl oz/½ cup) water and stir over low heat to dissolve the sugar. Boil for 5 minutes, or until reduced to 4 tablespoons, then set aside to cool. Strain the syrup and add the passionfruit pulp.

Peel and seed the pawpaw and melon. Cut the pawpaw and the melon into 4 cm (1½ in) cubes. Peel the mango and cut the flesh into cubes, discarding the stone. Peel, halve and core the pineapple and cut into cubes. Peel the lychees, then make a slit in the flesh and remove the seed.

Place all the fruit in a large serving bowl. Pour the syrup over the fruit, or serve separately, if you prefer. Garnish with the mint.

HINT:
• Serve with gluten-free low-fat yoghurt for a calcium boost.

BAKING

WALNUT AND SEED BREAD

3 eggs, lightly beaten

3 tbsp canola or olive oil

500 g (1 lb 2 oz/4 cups) soy-containing, gluten-free plain (all-purpose) flour

1 tsp soft brown sugar

2 tsp dried yeast GF

½ tsp salt

¼ tsp tartaric acid

1 tbsp each of sunflower seeds, pepitas and poppy seeds

85 g (3 oz/⅔ cup) chopped walnuts

canola or olive oil, extra, for glazing

mixed seeds, to sprinkle

PREP TIME: 30 MINUTES + 50 MINUTES RISING

COOKING TIME: 45 MINUTES

SERVES 8–10

Preheat the oven to 200°C (400°F/Gas 6). Lightly grease a 23 cm (9 in) round cake tin and line the base with baking paper.

Beat together the eggs, oil and 500 ml (17 fl oz/2 cups) warm water in a bowl. Put the flour, sugar, yeast, salt and tartaric acid in a separate large bowl. Using electric beaters, beat on a low speed for 20 seconds to combine. With the motor running, gradually beat in the egg mixture until smooth. Continue to beat for 5 minutes. Add the seeds and chopped walnuts and beat until incorporated.

Pour the batter into the prepared tin. Cover with greased plastic wrap and set aside in a warm place for 50 minutes until the batter has nearly risen to the top of the tin. Brush the top of the loaf lightly with oil and sprinkle evenly with the extra seeds. Bake for 45 minutes, or until golden brown.

Cool in the tin for 10 minutes, then turn out onto a wire rack to cool completely. Cut into slices to serve.

HINTS:
- When making this bread it's important to use a gluten-free flour mixture that includes soy flour in its composition. Soy flour acts more like gluten flour and gives a better result for the bread.
- Gluten-free yeast should be stored in the freezer.
- Gluten-free breads can sink after being taken out of the oven if the kitchen is too humid or if the bread was left to rise too long before being placed in the oven. If you make a yeast-leavened dough that doesn't rise properly, make it again and add 1 teaspoon of vinegar or a pinch of citric acid to the water before you add the yeast.
- Store the bread in an airtight container in the refrigerator for up to 5 days.

MANY PEOPLE FIND THEY MISS
WHOLEGRAIN BREAD AFTER
THEY START A GLUTEN-FREE
DIET. THIS RECIPE GIVES YOU
A GLUTEN-FREE BREAD THAT
HAS SOME TEXTURE AND BITE
TO IT. THE SEEDS AND NUTS
ADD FIBRE AND MINERALS.

nutrition per slice (10)

Energy 1193 kJ (284 Cal)
Fat 14.8 g
Saturated fat 1.7 g
Protein 4.4 g
Carbohydrate 33.1 g
Fibre 2 g
Cholesterol 56 mg

153

WHITE BREAD

ENJOY THE SMELL OF BREAD BAKING IN THE OVEN AND MAKE THIS GLUTEN-FREE VERSION OF WHITE BREAD. YOU CAN ADD MORE FIBRE TO THIS LOAF BY ADDING RICE BRAN TO THE DRY INGREDIENTS.

500 ml (17 fl oz/2 cups) milk
4 tsp dried yeast GF
1 tbsp sugar
550 g (1 lb 4 oz/3²⁄₃ cups) gluten-free plain
  (all-purpose) flour
2 tsp salt
4 tbsp canola or olive oil
1 egg

2 tbsp roasted buckwheat kernels (groats)
 (optional)
2 tbsp canola or olive oil, extra, for glazing

PREP TIME: 40 MINUTES
COOKING TIME: 55 MINUTES
SERVES 8–10

Preheat the oven to 220°C (425°F/Gas 7). Lightly grease a 20 x 14 cm (8 x 5½ in) loaf tin.

Pour the milk into a saucepan over medium heat, bring almost to the boil, then remove from the heat and allow to cool until it is lukewarm.

Combine the yeast, sugar and the warm milk in a bowl, then stir to dissolve the yeast. Stand the bowl in a warm place for about 10 minutes, or until the mixture is frothy.

Sift the flour into a large bowl and add the salt. Make a well in the centre and add the yeast mixture, oil and egg. Beat well with a wooden spoon. Pour into the prepared tin and sprinkle with buckwheat, if using. Cover loosely and place in a warm place for about 20 minutes, or until the mixture comes to the top of the tin.

Bake for 20 minutes, then reduce the heat to 200°C (400°F/Gas 6) and bake for a further 30–35 minutes, or until cooked. Brush with the extra oil during cooking at least twice to help promote browning.

HINTS:
• Store gluten-free yeast in the freezer.
• Use a commercial gluten-free bread mixture or flour mixture that's suitable for bread-making rather than one type of gluten-free flour—the result will be much better.
• To add more fibre to this loaf, add 40 g (1½ oz/½ cup) rice bran with the flour.
• Home-made bread is best eaten on the day of baking; alternatively, you can slice it, then freeze until required.

nutrition per slice (10): Energy 1495 kJ (357 Cal); Fat 13.8 g; Saturated fat 2.6 g; Protein 3.5 g; Carbohydrate 53.6 g; Fibre 1.2 g; Cholesterol 25 mg

SAVOURY FLAT BREAD

THIS BREAD IS GREAT FOR CHILDREN AND TEENAGERS WHO NEED A GLUTEN-
FREE DIET AS IT MAKES A GOOD GLUTEN-FREE ALTERNATIVE TO CRACKERS
AND PITA BREAD—PERFECT FOR SNACKS OR SCHOOL LUNCH BOXES.

80 g (2¾ oz/½ cup) brown rice flour
55 g (2 oz/½ cup) arrowroot
¾ tsp bicarbonate of soda (baking soda)
1½ tsp cream of tartar
100 g (3½ oz/1 cup) rice bran
250 ml (9 fl oz/1 cup) chicken stock GF
   (Basics) or water
3 tbsp canola or olive oil

canola or olive oil, extra, for glazing
1 tbsp salt
1 tbsp poppy seeds

PREP TIME: 20 MINUTES
COOKING TIME: 40 MINUTES
MAKES 6–8 ROUNDS

Preheat the oven to 190°C (375°F/Gas 5). Grease two baking trays.

Sift the flour, arrowroot, bicarbonate of soda and cream of tartar into a large bowl. Add the rice bran. Make a well in the centre, then add the combined stock and oil. Beat until smooth with a wooden spoon.

Spoon heaped tablespoons of the dough onto the prepared trays.

Bake for 20 minutes. Remove from the oven, brush with oil and sprinkle with salt and poppy seeds. Return to the oven and bake for a further 15–20 minutes.

HINTS:
• Many commercial stocks contain gluten so check the label.
• The bread can be topped or split and filled. It does not freeze well but can be kept in the refrigerator for 2–3 days.

nutrition per round (8): Energy 806 kJ (193 Cal); Fat 11.5 g; Saturated fat 1.4 g; Protein 3.2 g; Carbohydrate 17.2 g; Fibre 4 g; Cholesterol 1 mg

IF YOUR LOCAL SHOPS DON'T
SELL GLUTEN-FREE BREAD
ROLLS, THEN WHY NOT MAKE
YOUR OWN? MAKE A DOUBLE
BATCH AND FREEZE THEM
UNTIL NEEDED.

nutrition per roll

Energy 1300 kJ (311 Cal)
Fat 10.4 g
Saturated fat 4.6 g
Protein 3.1 g
Carbohydrate 48.8 g
Fibre 3.3 g
Cholesterol 19 mg

BREAD ROLLS

4 tsp dried yeast GF

1 tbsp soft brown sugar

2 tsp guar gum or xanthan gum

300 g (10½ oz/2 cups) gluten-free plain (all-purpose) flour

135 g (4¾ oz/¾ cup) rice flour

2 tsp salt

40 g (1½ oz/½ cup) rice bran

60 g (2¼ oz) butter, melted, cooled

2 tbsp poppy seeds or sesame seeds (optional)

canola or olive oil, for brushing

PREP TIME: 40 MINUTES + RISING TIME

COOKING TIME: 35 MINUTES

MAKES 8

Preheat the oven to 200°C (400°F/Gas 6). Lightly grease eight 10 x 5.5 cm (4 x 2¼ in) individual loaf tins.

Combine the yeast, sugar and 500 ml (17 fl oz/2 cups) warm water in a bowl, then stir to dissolve the yeast. Stand the bowl in a warm place for about 10 minutes, or until the mixture is frothy.

Sift the gum and flours into a large bowl. Add the salt and rice bran. Make a well in the centre and add the yeast mixture and cooled butter. Mix well to form a soft dough. Divide into eight equal portions, then gently shape with gluten-free floured hands into an oval shape. Place in the prepared tins. Sprinkle with poppy seeds or sesame seeds, if using.

Cover loosely and place in a warm place for 45–60 minutes, or until the mixture comes to the top of the tins.

Bake for 25–30 minutes, or until cooked through. Brush with oil during cooking at least twice to help promote browning. Remove from the tins and leave to cool on a wire rack.

HINTS:
• Store gluten-free yeast in the freezer.
• Guar gum and xanthan gum are available from health-food stores and some local coeliac organizations. These are useful products because they mimic the properties of gluten and help reduce crumbling in baked goods.
• The bread rolls are best eaten on the day they are made, but they can be frozen for up to 2 months.

CHEESE PINWHEELS

THESE GLUTEN-FREE PINWHEELS ARE A GOOD ALTERNATIVE TO SAVOURY
SCROLLS AND WILL HELP SATISFY A CRAVING FOR SOMETHING CHEESY OR
SAVOURY. THEY ARE A GOOD ADDITION TO LUNCH BOXES OR PICNIC HAMPERS.

120 g (4¼ oz/¾ cup) potato flour
175 g (6 oz/1 cup) rice flour
2 tsp gluten-free baking powder
85 g (3 oz) butter
3–4 tbsp milk
milk or water, for glazing
1 tbsp poppy seeds

RICOTTA FILLING
185 g (6½ oz/¾ cup) ricotta cheese
2 spring onions (scallions), finely chopped

PREP TIME: 20 MINUTES
COOKING TIME: 15 MINUTES
SERVES 4–6

Preheat the oven to 180°C (350°F/Gas 4). Lightly grease a 20 cm (8 in) sandwich tin.

Sift the dry ingredients into a bowl. Rub the butter in with your fingertips until the mixture resembles fine breadcrumbs. Make a well in the centre. Add enough milk to make a soft dough. Turn out onto a rice-floured board and knead lightly.

Roll the dough into a 5 mm (¼ in) thick rectangle between two sheets of baking paper. Turn and release the paper frequently to prevent the dough from sticking to the paper.

To make the ricotta filling, beat the ricotta cheese in a bowl until creamy. Add the spring onions and mix well. Spread the filling over the dough.

Use the baking paper to help you roll up the dough. Once you have a roll, cut it into 2 cm (¾ in) thick slices. Place the slices, cut side up, into the prepared tin. Glaze with milk or water and sprinkle the top with poppy seeds. Bake for 12–15 minutes. Serve hot or cold.

nutrition per serve (6): Energy 1467 kJ (350 Cal); Fat 17 g; Saturated fat 10.5 g; Protein 7.4 g; Carbohydrate 40.1 g; Fibre 2.4 g; Cholesterol 53 mg

SCONES

JUST BECAUSE YOU FOLLOW A GLUTEN-FREE DIET DOESN'T MEAN YOU CAN'T ENJOY A TRADITIONAL AFTERNOON TEA. THIS RECIPE GIVES YOU A GLUTEN-FREE VERSION OF SCONES. SERVE WITH JAM AND CREAM, HOT OR COLD.

550 g (1 lb 4 oz/3⅔ cups) gluten-free
  self-raising flour
3 tsp gluten-free baking powder
80 g (2¾ oz) butter, softened
1 tbsp caster (superfine) sugar
310 ml (10¾ fl oz/1¼ cups) milk

whipped cream, to serve
strawberry jam GF (Basics), to serve

PREP TIME: 10 MINUTES
COOKING TIME: 15 MINUTES
MAKES 12

Preheat the oven to 220°C (425°F/Gas 7). Line a baking tray with a sheet of baking paper.

Sift the flour, baking powder and a pinch of salt into a large bowl. Use your fingertips to rub the butter into the flour until it resembles fine breadcrumbs. Stir in the sugar. Add the milk and use a round-bladed knife to mix until the dough just comes together.

Turn out onto a surface lightly dusted with gluten-free flour and knead until combined. Press or roll out until the dough is about 2 cm (¾ in) thick. Use a 5.5 cm (2¼ in) round cutter to cut out the dough. Place on the lined tray about 1 cm (½ in) apart. Re-roll and cut any remaining dough.

Bake for 12–15 minutes, or until cooked. Serve warm with lashings of whipped cream and strawberry jam.

HINTS:
• Look for a gluten-free flour mixture that is suitable for baked goods (check the information on the packet). You will get a better result than by using a gluten-free flour made up of only one type of flour.
• If you're lactose intolerant, replace the milk with rice drink or soy milk and make sure to buy a gluten-free flour mixture that doesn't contain milk powder.
• If you're invited to an afternoon tea at a friend's house, take a container of these scones with you, so you have something suitable to eat.

nutrition per scone: Energy 999 kJ (239 Cal); Fat 6.8 g; Saturated fat 4.3 g; Protein 1.6 g; Carbohydrate 42.7 g; Fibre 4.8 g; Cholesterol 20 mg

SAVOURY CORN AND CHIVE MUFFINS

300 g (10½ oz/2 cups) gluten-free
   self-raising flour
2 tsp gluten-free baking powder
2 tbsp soft brown sugar
100 g (3½ oz/½ cup) drained, tinned corn
   kernels
2 tbsp finely chopped fresh chives
250 ml (9 fl oz/1 cup) milk

4 tbsp canola or olive oil
2 eggs, lightly beaten

PREP TIME: 15 MINUTES
COOKING TIME: 20 MINUTES
MAKES 10

Preheat the oven to 180°C (350°F/Gas 4). Lightly grease 10 holes of a regular muffin tin.

Sift the flour and baking powder into a large bowl. Stir in the sugar, corn and chives, then make a well in the centre. In a separate bowl, combine the milk, oil and eggs. Pour into the well in the dry ingredients. Use a large metal spoon to mix until just combined. Divide the batter evenly among the prepared muffin holes.

Bake for 18–20 minutes, or until a skewer inserted in the centre comes out clean. Leave in the tray for 5 minutes before turning out onto a wire rack to cool.

HINTS:
• A combination of gluten-free flours usually produces a better product than using only one type of flour. This is why many commercial gluten-free flour mixtures contain a number of different flours.
• If you're lactose intolerant, replace the milk with rice drink or gluten-free soy milk.
• Like many gluten-free baked goods, these muffins don't stay fresh for very long. They need to be eaten on the day they are made or they can be frozen for up to 1 month.

IT'S OFTEN HARD TO FIND GLUTEN-
FREE FOOD WHEN YOU'RE ON THE
MOVE, SO BE PREPARED TO EAT
WELL BY TAKING SUITABLE FOODS
WITH YOU. THESE LITTLE MUFFINS
ARE PERFECT BECAUSE THEY ARE
LIGHT AND PORTABLE.

nutrition per muffin   Energy 948 kJ (226 Cal)

Fat 10 g

Saturated fat 1.5 g

Protein 3.9 g

Carbohydrate 29.4 g

Fibre 3.8 g

Cholesterol 41 mg

PIKELETS

PIKELETS MAKE A GREAT AFTERNOON TEA AT THE END OF A SCHOOL DAY OR ON A LAZY WEEKEND. HUNGRY KIDS AND TEENAGERS WILL REALLY APPRECIATE THEM.

115 g (4 oz/¾ cup) gluten-free plain
  (all-purpose) flour
½ tsp bicarbonate of soda (baking soda)
1 tsp cream of tartar
4 tbsp rice bran
2 eggs, separated
1 tbsp canola oil
strawberry jam GF (Basics), to serve

PREP TIME: 15 MINUTES
COOKING TIME: 25 MINUTES
MAKES ABOUT 24

Sift the flour, bicarbonate of soda and cream of tartar into a bowl. Mix in the rice bran. Make a well in the centre. In a separate bowl, combine the egg yolks, oil and 250 ml (9 fl oz/1 cup) water. Add to the well in the dry ingredients. Beat well until smooth.

Beat the egg whites in the small bowl of an electric mixer until stiff peaks form, then fold into the batter using a large spoon.

Spray a non-stick frying pan lightly with canola or olive oil and place over medium heat. Place tablespoonfuls of the mixture in the pan, allowing room for spreading. When the mixture starts to set and bubbles burst, turn over and brown the other side. Place on a wire rack to cool. Repeat with the remaining mixture. Serve the warm pikelets topped with strawberry jam.

HINTS:
• Pikelets can be frozen. When ready to eat, thaw them, then reheat briefly in a warm oven.
• Experiment with different toppings for the pikelets, such as maple syrup, honey, pure fruit jam or your favourite spread.

nutrition per pikelet: Energy 151 kJ (36 Cal); Fat 1.5 g; Saturated fat 0.2 g; Protein 0.8 g; Carbohydrate 4.6 g; Fibre 0.4 g; Cholesterol 16 mg

JAM COOKIES

BE PREPARED TO COOK LOTS OF THESE—YOU MIGHT NOT BE ABLE TO MAKE THESE COOKIES FAST ENOUGH TO KEEP UP WITH THE DEMAND.

90 g (3¼ oz) **unsalted butter**
110 g (3¾ oz/½ cup) **sugar**
125 g (4½ oz/¾ cup) **rice flour**
¼ tsp **gluten-free baking powder**
165 g (5¾ oz/½ cup) **strawberry jam** GF
   (Basics)

PREP TIME: 20 MINUTES
COOKING TIME: 15 MINUTES
MAKES ABOUT 24

Preheat the oven to 190°C (375°F/Gas 5). Lightly grease two baking trays.

Use electric beaters to beat the butter and sugar until light and fluffy. Sift in the flour and baking powder, then stir together. Add 1 tablespoon water and stir until well blended and a dough forms.

Shape the dough into walnut-sized balls, then space them out on the prepared baking trays—you should have about 24 balls.

Make an indentation in each cookie using the handle of a wooden spoon. Put ¼ teaspoon jam in each biscuit. Bake for 10–15 minutes, or until light golden. Cool on wire racks.

HINTS:
• You may find the dough easier to work with if you refrigerate it for 30 minutes before rolling the dough into balls.
• The dough can be made ahead of time and stored, covered, in the refrigerator for 2–3 days before baking.
• For a special treat, you can add 80 g (2¾ oz/½ cup) gluten-free choc chips to the dough mixture for jam and choc chip cookies.

nutrition per cookie: Energy 311 kJ (74 Cal); Fat 3.2 g; Saturated fat 2 g; Protein 0.4 g; Carbohydrate 11.2 g; Fibre 0.2 g; Cholesterol 10 mg

ONCE YOU'VE COOKED THESE COOKIES A FEW TIMES YOU MAY WANT TO START EXPERIMENTING BY ADDING NUTS, CHOCOLATE, CAROB OR EVEN DRIED FRUIT TO THE BASIC MIXTURE.

nutrition per cookie

Energy 464 kJ (111 Cal)
Fat 5.9 g
Saturated fat 3.8 g
Protein 0.5 g
Carbohydrate 13.8 g
Fibre 0.4 g
Cholesterol 18 mg

VANILLA COOKIES

125 g (4½ oz) **unsalted butter**
4 tbsp **caster (superfine) sugar**
1 tsp **natural vanilla extract**
150 g (5½ oz/1 cup) **gluten-free plain
    (all-purpose) flour**
70 g (2½ oz/½ cup) **gluten-free self-raising
    flour**

PREP TIME: 15 MINUTES
COOKING TIME: 15 MINUTES
MAKES ABOUT 18

Preheat the oven to 170°C (325°F/Gas 3). Line two baking trays with baking paper.

Beat the butter, sugar and vanilla extract in the small bowl of an electric mixer for
1–2 minutes, or until well combined. Sift the flours into the butter mixture. Use a wooden
spoon to mix until well combined. Use your hands to shape the mixture into a soft dough.

Shape tablespoons of the mixture into balls and place on the prepared trays. Use a fork to
flatten the balls until about 1 cm (⅜ in) thick. Bake for 12–15 minutes, swapping the trays
around once, until light golden. Transfer the cookies to a wire rack to cool.

HINTS:
• Make sure you store gluten-free flours separately from gluten-containing flours, in
  labelled containers, to avoid cross-contamination. Brown rice flour and soya flour should
  be stored in the refrigerator, whereas other gluten-free flours can be stored in a cool
  dark place. For long-term storage, keep gluten-free flours in the freezer in well-sealed
  containers. The flour doesn't need to be thawed before being used.
• You may find the dough easier to work with if you refrigerate it for 30 minutes before
  shaping the dough into balls.
• If you like, you can add 100 g (3½ oz) chopped gluten-free chocolate, carob, nuts or
  dried fruit to the dough before mixing it together with a wooden spoon.

APPLE SLICE

THIS SLICE IS DELICIOUS FOR MORNING OR AFTERNOON TEA. MAKE SURE YOU USE PURE GLUTEN-FREE ICING SUGAR TO DUST THE SLICE. SOFT ICING SUGAR AND ICING SUGAR MIXTURES MAY CONTAIN GLUTEN.

220 g (7¾ oz/1½ cups) gluten-free
   self-raising flour
½ tsp gluten-free baking powder
175 g (6 oz/¾ cup) caster (superfine) sugar
2 eggs, lightly beaten
3 tbsp apple juice
3 tbsp canola oil
335 g (11¾ oz/1½ cups) unsweetened
   stewed apples
pure icing (confectioners') sugar GF,
   to serve

PREP TIME: 15 MINUTES
COOKING TIME: 35 MINUTES
MAKES ABOUT 20 PIECES

Preheat the oven to 190°C (375°F/Gas 5). Lightly grease a 28 x 18 cm (11¼ x 7 in) baking tin and cover the base and two long sides with baking paper.

Sift the flour and baking powder into a bowl and add the sugar. Make a well in the centre. Combine the eggs, juice, oil and 125 ml (4 fl oz/½ cup) cold water in a separate bowl, then add to the dry ingredients. Mix until thoroughly combined.

Spread half the batter into the prepared tin. Spread the stewed apple carefully over the top, then spoon the remaining batter gently over the apple so that it is completely covered.

Bake for 30–35 minutes, or until golden. Cool slightly in the tin, then place on a wire rack to cool completely. Dust with icing sugar and cut into 20 pieces before serving.

HINTS:
• Check that you are using pure icing sugar; some icing sugar mixtures contain gluten.
• You can make a pear version of this slice by replacing the apple with 4 tinned pear halves that have been mashed, and replacing the apple juice with pear juice.

nutrition per serve: Energy 475 kJ (113 Cal); Fat 3.6 g; Saturated fat 0.4 g; Protein 1.6 g; Carbohydrate 18.3 g; Fibre 0.9 g; Cholesterol 19 mg

RHUBARB MUFFINS

WITH GLUTEN-FREE FLOURS READILY AVAILABLE IN SUPERMARKETS, IT'S EASY TO MAKE YOUR OWN HOME-MADE MUFFINS. MAKE A BATCH AND FREEZE THEM SO YOU HAVE A READY SUPPLY OF GLUTEN-FREE SNACKS.

300 g (10½ oz/2 cups) gluten-free
    self-raising flour
2 tsp gluten-free baking powder
140 g (5 oz/¾ cup) soft brown sugar
185 ml (6 fl oz/¾ cup) milk
4 tbsp canola oil
2 eggs, lightly beaten
200 g (7 oz/½ bunch) trimmed rhubarb,
    washed and cut into 2 cm (¾ in) pieces

PREP TIME: 15 MINUTES
COOKING TIME: 20 MINUTES
MAKES 12

Preheat the oven to 180°C (350°F/Gas 4). Lightly grease 12 holes of a regular muffin tray.

Sift the flour and baking powder into a large bowl. Stir in the sugar and make a well in the centre. In a separate bowl, combine the milk, oil and eggs. Pour into the well in the dry ingredients along with the rhubarb. Use a large metal spoon to mix until just combined. Divide the batter evenly among the prepared muffin holes.

Bake for 18–20 minutes, or until a skewer inserted in the centre comes out clean. Leave to cool in the tin for 5 minutes before turning out onto a wire rack to cool completely.

HINTS:
• These muffins are best eaten on the day they are made but they can be frozen for up to 1 month.
• If you are lactose intolerant replace the milk with rice drink or gluten-free soy milk.

nutrition per muffin: Energy 903 kJ (216 Cal); Fat 8.4 g; Saturated fat 1.2 g; Protein 3.8 g; Carbohydrate 30.2 g; Fibre 1.8 g; Cholesterol 33 mg

MIXED BERRY MUFFINS

300 g (10½ oz/2 cups) gluten-free plain
   (all-purpose) flour
1 tbsp gluten-free baking powder
25 g (1 oz/½ cup) baby rice cereal or rice
   porridge
150 g (5½ oz/⅔ cup) caster (superfine)
   sugar
2 eggs, lightly beaten
375 ml (13 fl oz/1½ cups) reduced-fat milk

2 tbsp canola oil
250 g (9 oz/1⅔ cups) fresh or frozen mixed
   berries

PREP TIME: 15 MINUTES
COOKING TIME: 20 MINUTES
MAKES 12

Preheat oven to 200°C (400°F/Gas 6). Lightly grease 12 holes of a regular muffin tray.

Sift the flour and baking powder into a large bowl. Stir in the rice cereal and sugar and make a well in the centre. In a separate bowl combine the beaten eggs, milk and oil. Pour the mixture into the well in the dry ingredients and stir briefly until the batter is just incorporated. Quickly and lightly stir through the berries. Do not over-mix. Divide the batter evenly among the prepared muffin holes.

Bake for 20 minutes, or until golden brown and risen. Leave in the tray for 5 minutes before turning out onto a wire rack to cool completely.

HINTS:
• Use dried fruit such as chopped dates, sultanas, raisins or apricots instead of the berries, if you prefer.
• If you are making these muffins for someone with diabetes, you can lower the muffins' GI by using sucralose instead of sugar. Similarly, if making these muffins for someone with lactose intolerance, use gluten-free soy milk or rice milk instead of cow's milk.

IF YOU HAVE YOUNG CHILDREN
WHO NEED A GLUTEN-FREE DIET,
YOU CAN MAKE BITE-SIZED
MUFFINS USING A MINI MUFFIN
PAN. THAT WAY, YOU'LL WASTE
LESS IF YOUR CHILD CAN'T EAT A
WHOLE REGULAR-SIZED MUFFIN.

nutrition per muffin

Energy 882 kJ (211 Cal)
Fat 4.6 g
Saturated fat 0.8 g
Protein 3.3 g
Carbohydrate 38.8 g
Fibre 0.9 g
Cholesterol 34 mg

COFFEE MOUSSE MERINGUE ROLL

THIS IS SIMILAR TO A SWISS (JELLY) ROLL USING MERINGUE INSTEAD OF CAKE. THE SOPHISTICATED COFFEE MOUSSE MAKES A DELICIOUS FILLING.

COFFEE MOUSSE

4 egg yolks

3 tbsp sugar

3 tsp pure maize cornflour (cornstarch) GF

1½ tsp instant coffee powder

pure maize cornflour (cornstarch) GF, for dusting

4 egg whites

110 g (3¾ oz/½ cup) sugar

2 tsp pure maize cornflour (cornstarch) GF

pure icing (confectioners') sugar GF, for dusting

PREP TIME: 35 MINUTES

COOKING TIME: 15 MINUTES

SERVES 4–6

To make the coffee mousse, beat the egg yolks and sugar in the small bowl of an electric mixer until thick and creamy. In a separate small bowl, blend the cornflour, coffee powder and 185 ml (6 fl oz/¾ cup) water. Add to the egg mixture. Transfer to a saucepan and stir over low heat until the mixture boils and thickens. Pour the mixture into a bowl. Cover with plastic wrap and chill well before using.

Preheat the oven to 200°C (400°F/Gas 6). Lightly grease a 25 x 30 cm (10 x 12 in) Swiss roll (jelly roll) tin, line with baking paper, grease again and dust with cornflour.

Beat the egg whites until light and fluffy. Gradually beat in the sugar and continue beating until the meringue is stiff and glossy. Gently fold in the cornflour. Spread the meringue mixture evenly into the prepared Swiss roll tin, using a spatula.

Bake for 12–15 minutes, or until the meringue has risen and is golden brown. Quickly turn out onto a sheet of baking paper that has been coated with sifted pure icing sugar. Allow to cool until lukewarm.

Spread the mousse over the meringue. Roll up from the short side using the baking paper as a guide. Place on a chilled platter. Refrigerate the roll until ready to serve, then slice.

HINT:
• If you have diabetes, you can use sucralose instead of sugar to lower the GI.

nutrition per serve: Energy 661 kJ (158 Cal); Fat 3.2 g; Saturated fat 1 g; Protein 4.1 g; Carbohydrate 29.3 g; Fibre 0.1 g; Cholesterol 119 mg

PUMPKIN AND COCONUT TART

THIS TART IS GREAT TO SHARE WITH FRIENDS FOR MORNING OR AFTERNOON TEA, OR YOU COULD EVEN SERVE IT FOR DESSERT WITH SOME ICE CREAM.

1 quantity gluten-free sweet shortcrust pastry (Basics)

375 g (13 oz/1½ cups) cooked mashed butternut pumpkin (squash)

3 eggs, lightly beaten

165 g (5¾ oz/¾ cup firmly packed) soft brown sugar

125 g (4½ oz/½ cup) sour cream

30 g (1 oz/½ cup) flaked coconut

3 tbsp golden syrup or pure maple syrup

pure icing (confectioners') sugar GF, to dust

PREP TIME: 25 MINUTES

COOKING TIME: 1¼ HOURS

SERVES 8–10

Preheat the oven to 200°C (400°F/Gas 6). Lightly grease a 23 cm (9 in) loose-based flan tin.

Roll out the pastry between two sheets of baking paper until large enough to line the prepared tin. Reserve any leftover dough.

Place the tin on a baking tray. Cover the pastry with a sheet of crumpled baking paper and fill with baking beads or rice. Bake for 10 minutes. Remove the beads and paper and bake for a further 10–15 minutes, or until lightly browned. Fill any cracks with small amounts of reserved pastry. Bake for a further 2 minutes to set. Remove from the oven and cool completely. Reduce the oven temperature to 180°C (350°F/Gas 4).

To make the filling, combine all the ingredients (except the icing sugar) in a large bowl and mix together well. Place the cooled pastry case on a baking tray and pour in the filling.

Bake for 45 minutes; or until the filling is just set. Cool completely before serving. Dust the edges lightly with icing sugar.

HINT:
• Make sure you use pure icing sugar to dust the tart. Soft icing sugar or icing sugar mixtures can contain cornflour with wheat starch in it.

nutrition per serve (10): Energy 1348 kJ (322 Cal); Fat 14.7 g; Saturated fat 9.1 g; Protein 4.1 g; Carbohydrate 44.1 g; Fibre 1 g; Cholesterol 112 mg

THESE LITTLE GEMS ARE GREAT
FOR PARTIES AND CERTAINLY
DON'T FEEL LIKE SPECIAL DIET
FOOD. THE MERINGUE KISSES CAN
BE DIPPED IN MELTED CHOCOLATE
OR CAROB OR JOINED TOGETHER
WITH WHIPPED CREAM. THEY'RE
SURE TO IMPRESS.

nutrition per meringue   Energy 128 kJ (31 Cal)
Fat 0 g
Saturated fat 0 g
Protein 0.3 g
Carbohydrate 7.6 g
Fibre 0 g
Cholesterol 0 mg

MERINGUE KISSES

pure maize cornflour (cornstarch) GF, for dusting
2 egg whites
150 g (5½ oz/⅔ cup) caster (superfine) sugar
1 tsp pure icing (confectioners') sugar GF

PREP TIME: 20 MINUTES
COOKING TIME: 40 MINUTES
MAKES ABOUT 20

Preheat the oven to 120°C (235°F/Gas ½). Lightly grease two baking trays, then dust them lightly with cornflour.

Combine the egg whites, caster sugar and a pinch of salt in the small bowl of an electric mixer. Beat on high speed for 10–12 minutes. Gently fold in the icing sugar.

Spoon the meringue into a piping bag fitted with a fluted tube. Pipe stars or rosettes onto the prepared trays. Bake for about 40 minutes, or until the meringues feel firm and dry. Leave to cool in the oven with the door ajar.

HINTS:
• Make sure you use pure icing sugar. Soft icing sugar or icing sugar mixtures can contain cornflour with wheat starch in it.
• This basic meringue mixture makes small, crisp meringues that store well in an airtight container for a few days. For the best result, make sure that you have enough egg white to fully absorb the sugar.
• Once cooled, the meringue kisses can be dipped in melted gluten-free chocolate or carob. They can also be joined together with whipped cream.

BANANA LOAF

BANANA BREAD IS A REAL CROWD PLEASER AND IS DELICIOUS WARM, TOASTED OR COLD. SERVE IT FOR AFTERNOON TEA OR TOAST IT FOR A DELICIOUS BREAKFAST.

300 g (10½ oz/2 cups) gluten-free
  self-raising flour
2 tsp gluten-free baking powder
125 g (4½ oz/⅔ cup) soft brown sugar
¼ tsp ground cinnamon
125 g (4½ oz) butter, melted, cooled
  slightly
125 ml (4 fl oz/½ cup) milk
2 eggs

3 large (700 g/1 lb 9 oz) ripe bananas,
  mashed
butter, to serve
maple syrup, to serve

PREP TIME: 20 MINUTES
COOKING TIME: 50 MINUTES
SERVES 8

Preheat the oven to 170°C (325°F/Gas 3). Grease a 21 x 11 cm (8¼ x 4¼ in) loaf tin. Line the base of the tin with baking paper.

Sift the flour, baking powder, sugar and cinnamon into a large bowl. In a separate bowl, whisk the butter, milk and egg together. Add the milk mixture to the dry ingredients with the mashed bananas. Use a wooden spoon to mix until well combined.

Pour the mixture into the prepared tin and smooth the surface with a spoon. Bake for 40 minutes, or until a skewer inserted into the centre comes out clean. Set aside in the tin for 5 minutes before turning out onto a wire rack to cool. Serve warm or at room temperature. Cut into slices, spread with butter and drizzle with a little maple syrup.

HINTS:
• Spread the slices with a little low-fat ricotta cheese before drizzling with syrup.
• This loaf is best eaten on the day it is made.
• If you're lactose intolerant or catering for someone who is, then replace the milk with rice drink or gluten-free soy milk.
• When baking gluten-free goods, use heavy-duty tins rather than aluminium; this will help them cook evenly.

nutrition per serve: Energy 1588 kJ (379 Cal); Fat 15.9 g; Saturated fat 9.4 g; Protein 6.1 g; Carbohydrate 51.5 g; Fibre 3.3 g; Cholesterol 89 mg

PATTY CAKES

THESE SWEET LITTLE CAKES ARE READY IN A FLASH AND ARE GREAT FOR CHILDREN'S PARTIES, ESPECIALLY WHEN DECORATED WITH GLUTEN-FREE ICING AND CONFECTIONERY.

125 g (4½ oz) butter
115 g (4 oz/½ cup) caster (superfine) sugar
2 eggs, or equivalent egg replacer
150 g (5½ oz/1 cup) gluten-free self-raising flour
90 g (3¼ oz/½ cup) rice flour
3 tsp gluten-free baking powder

125 ml (4 fl oz/½ cup) milk
pure icing (confectioners') sugar GF, for dusting

PREP TIME: 15 MINUTES
COOKING TIME: 20 MINUTES
MAKES 24

Preheat the oven to 180°C (350°F/Gas 4). Line 12 holes of two regular muffin trays or patty pans with paper cases.

In the small bowl of an electric mixer, beat the butter and sugar together until light and fluffy. Add the eggs, one at a time, beating well after each addition.

Sift the dry ingredients into a large bowl. Fold the dry ingredients into the butter mixture alternately with the milk.

Spoon the mixture evenly into the muffin holes and bake for about 15–20 minutes, or until just cooked. Cool on a wire rack. Dust the patty cakes with pure icing sugar before serving. Alternatively, leave off the icing sugar and top the cakes with gluten-free icing (see below).

HINTS:
• For a dairy-free version, you can replace the butter with dairy-free margarine and the milk with gluten-free soy milk or rice drink.
• It's important to use pure icing sugar to ensure no gluten has been added.
• These can be iced with carob or cocoa icing: To make the icing, sift 185 g (6½ oz/ 1½ cups) pure icing (confectioners') sugar GF and 1 tablespoon unsweetened cocoa powder GF or carob powder into a heatproof bowl. Add enough cold water to make a smooth paste. Place the bowl over a saucepan of simmering water and stir continuously until the icing softens to the required consistency.

nutrition per cake: Energy 437 kJ (104 Cal); Fat 5.1 g; Saturated fat 3.1 g; Protein 1.5 g; Carbohydrate 12.9 g; Fibre 0.5 g; Cholesterol 30 mg

SPONGE CAKE

4 eggs
165 g (5¾ oz/¾ cup) sugar
150 g (5½ oz/1 cup) soy-free, gluten-free
plain (all-purpose) flour, sifted
100 g (3½ oz/⅓ cup) strawberry jam GF
(Basics)
pure icing (confectioners') sugar GF, to
serve
300 ml (10½ fl oz) pouring (whipping)
cream

PREP TIME: 20 MINUTES
COOKING TIME: 30 MINUTES
SERVES 6–8

Preheat the oven to 180°C (350°F/Gas 4). Lightly grease and flour two 20 cm (8 in) round cake tins, then line the base with baking paper.

Beat the eggs and sugar in the small bowl of an electric mixer for about 6–7 minutes, or until light and fluffy. Very gently fold the sifted flour into the egg mixture alternately with 4 tablespoons hot water. Gently spread the mixture into the prepared pans.

Bake for about 25–30 minutes, or until lightly browned and the cakes have slightly left the side of the tins. Turn onto a wire rack to cool.

Whip the cream into stiff peaks.

Spread the jam over the top of one sponge, and top with the cream. Place the other sponge on top and dust with icing sugar.

HINTS:
• This sponge has no wheat flour and no chemical raising agent, but relies on air for its lightness. Take great care when folding in dry ingredients. Use a large slotted metal spoon to ensure light, even folding.
• If you prefer, you can use apricot, peach or pear jam instead of strawberry.
• Since some icing sugar mixtures contain gluten, it's important to use pure icing sugar.
• If you are lactose intolerant, you can make mock whipped cream. To make the mock whipped cream, sprinkle 1 teaspoon powdered gelatine over 4 tablespoons cold water in a small heatproof bowl. Stand the bowl in a small saucepan of simmering water and stir until the gelatine has dissolved. Cool slightly. Beat 125 g (4½ oz) dairy-free margarine, 3 tablespoons caster (superfine) sugar and ½ teaspoon natural vanilla extract in a small bowl with electric beaters until pale in colour. Gradually add the cooled gelatine mixture and beat until light and fluffy.

GLUTEN-FREE COOKING HAS COME A LONG WAY. IT USED TO BE REALLY DIFFICULT TO MAKE A LIGHT, FLUFFY GLUTEN-FREE SPONGE, BUT NOW YOU CAN EASILY MAKE ONE AT HOME USING A GOOD QUALITY GLUTEN-FREE FLOUR MIXTURE.

nutrition per serve (8)

Energy 1477 kJ (353 Cal)
Fat 18.9 g
Saturated fat 11.5 g
Protein 4.3 g
Carbohydrate 42.7 g
Fibre 0.6 g
Cholesterol 123 mg

FLOURLESS CHOCOLATE WALNUT CAKE

THIS CAKE HAS NO FLOUR WHATSOEVER. FOR BEST RESULTS USE A PREMIUM BITTERSWEET DARK CHOCOLATE WITH A HIGH LEVEL OF COCOA SOLIDS.

125 g (4½ oz/1¼ cups) walnuts
250 g (9 oz) dark chocolate GF, chopped
2 tbsp pouring (whipping) cream
1 tsp natural vanilla extract
115 g (4 oz/½ cup) caster (superfine) sugar
6 eggs, separated
fresh raspberries, to serve
whipped cream, to serve

PREP TIME: 20 MINUTES
COOKING TIME: 40 MINUTES
SERVES 8

Preheat oven to 180°C (350°F/Gas 4). Grease and line the base of a 20 cm (8 in) spring-form cake tin with baking paper.

Process the walnuts in a food processor until finely ground.

Put the chocolate, cream and vanilla extract in a heatproof bowl. Sit over a saucepan half filled with simmering water. Turn off the heat and stir the chocolate until just melted. Allow the mixture to cool a little.

Add the sugar, egg yolks and ground walnuts to the chocolate mixture and mix to combine. Using electric beaters, beat the egg whites until firm peaks form. Stir a large spoonful of the egg white into the chocolate to soften the mixture, then fold through the remaining egg white. Pour into the prepared tin. Bake for 40 minutes or until firm to touch. Leave to cool for 5 minutes, then turn out onto a wire rack to cool completely. Serve with fresh raspberries and whipped cream.

HINTS:
• Replace the ground walnuts with hazelnut meal or almond meal, if you prefer.
• You can use reduced-fat cream to help lower the fat content.

nutrition per serve: Energy 1660 kJ (398 Cal); Fat 25.7 g; Saturated fat 8.6 g; Protein 8.7 g; Carbohydrate 34 g; Fibre 1.4 g; Cholesterol 149 mg

BIRTHDAY CAKE

A BIRTHDAY IS A SPECIAL OCCASION THAT DESERVES A TRULY SPECIAL CAKE—LIKE THIS ONE.

pure maize cornflour (cornstarch) GF,
   for dusting
6 eggs
220 g (7¾ oz/1 cup) sugar
4 tbsp arrowroot
4 tbsp pure maize cornflour (cornstarch) GF
165 g (5¾ oz/½ cup) strawberry jam GF
   (Basics)

MARSHMALLOW FROSTING
3 tsp powdered gelatine
500 g (1 lb 2 oz/2¼ cups) sugar

PREP TIME: 1½ HOURS
COOKING TIME: 45 MINUTES
SERVES 10–12

Preheat the oven to 180°C (350°F/Gas 4). Lightly grease three 23 cm (9 in) round sandwich tins or two 28 x 18 cm (11¼ x 7 in) tins, then dust with cornflour.

Combine the eggs and sugar in the bowl of an electric mixer. Beat until thick and light. Gently fold in the sifted arrowroot and cornflour. Divide the mixture among the three round tins or two rectangular tins.

Bake for 25–30 minutes, or until well risen and pale golden. Turn onto wire racks to cool.

Sandwich the cooled cakes together using the jam. Place the cake on a stiff board or plate.

To make the marshmallow frosting, dissolve the gelatine in 210 ml (7½ fl oz) water. Pour into a saucepan. Add 230 ml (7¾ fl oz) water and the sugar and mix well. Heat gently, stirring until boiling. Simmer without stirring over low heat for 15 minutes.

Remove the pan from the heat and leave to cool slightly. Scoop the frosting into the large bowl of an electric mixer and beat on high speed until the mixture doubles in bulk and becomes thick. Spread quickly over the cake, using a metal spatula.

HINT:
• Decorate the cake with your choice of gluten-free confectionery. You'll need to work quickly before the frosting sets.

nutrition per serve (12): Energy 1295 kJ (309 Cal); Fat 2.5 g; Saturated fat 0.8 g; Protein 4 g; Carbohydrate 70.3 g; Fibre 0.2 g; Cholesterol 94 mg

BASICS

BEEF STOCK

2 kg (4 lb 8 oz) beef bones
2 unpeeled carrots, chopped
2 unpeeled onions, quartered
2 tbsp tomato paste (concentrated purée) GF
2 celery stalks, leaves included, chopped
1 bouquet garni
12 black peppercorns

Preheat the oven to 210°C (415°F/Gas 6–7). Put the bones in a baking tin and bake for 30 minutes, turning occasionally. Add the carrot and onion and cook for a further 20 minutes. Allow to cool.

Put the bones, onion and carrot in a large, heavy-based saucepan. Drain the excess fat from the baking tin and pour 250 ml (9 fl oz/1 cup) water into the tin. Stir to dissolve any pan juices, then add the liquid to the pan.

Add the tomato paste, celery and 2.5 litres (87 fl oz/10 cups) water. Bring to the boil, skimming the surface as required, and then add the bouquet garni and peppercorns. Reduce the heat to low and simmer gently for 4 hours. Skim the froth from the surface regularly.

Strain through a colander, then through a fine sieve. Remove any fat from the surface. Store in the refrigerator for up to 2 days or in the freezer for up to 6 months. Makes about 1.75 litres (61 fl oz/7 cups).

HINT:
• To make your own bouquet garni, tie together with a string or wrap in a piece of cheesecloth (muslin) 4 sprigs parsley or chervil, 1 sprig fresh thyme and 1 bay leaf.

CHICKEN STOCK

2 kg (4 lb 8 oz) chicken bones
2 unpeeled onions, quartered
2 unpeeled carrots, chopped
2 celery stalks, leaves included, chopped
1 bouquet garni
12 black peppercorns

Put the chicken bones, onion, carrot, celery and 3.5 litres (122 fl oz/14 cups) water in a large, heavy-based saucepan. Bring slowly to the boil. Skim the surface as required and add the bouquet garni and peppercorns. Reduce the heat to low and simmer gently for 3 hours. Skim the froth from the surface regularly.

Strain the stock. Set aside to cool, then refrigerate until cold. Spoon off any fat that has set on the surface. Transfer to an airtight container. Store in the refrigerator for up to 2 days or in the freezer for up to 6 months. Makes about 2.5 litres (87 fl oz/10 cups).

HINT:
• To make your own bouquet garni, tie together with a string or wrap in a piece of cheesecloth (muslin) 4 sprigs parsley or chervil, 1 sprig fresh thyme and 1 bay leaf.

VEGETABLE STOCK

1 tbsp oil
1 onion, chopped
2 leeks, thickly sliced
4 carrots, chopped
2 parsnips, chopped

4 celery stalks, leaves included, chopped
2 bay leaves
1 bouquet garni
4 unpeeled garlic cloves
8 black peppercorns

Heat the oil in a large, heavy-based saucepan and add the onion, leek, carrot, parsnip and celery. Cover and cook for 5 minutes without colouring. Add 3 litres (105 fl oz/12 cups) water. Bring to the boil. Add the bay leaves, bouquet garni, garlic and peppercorns. Reduce the heat to low and simmer for 1 hour. Skim the froth from the surface of the stock regularly.

Strain the stock. Set aside to cool, then transfer to an airtight container. Store in the refrigerator for up to 2 days or in the freezer for up to 6 months. Makes about 2.5 litres (87 fl oz/10 cups).

HINT:
• To make your own bouquet garni, tie together with a string or wrap in a piece of cheesecloth (muslin) 4 sprigs parsley or chervil, 1 sprig fresh thyme and 1 bay leaf.

FISH STOCK

2 kg (4 lb 8 oz) chopped fish bones, heads and tails
1 celery stalk, leaves included, roughly chopped
1 onion, chopped
1 unpeeled carrot, chopped
1 leek, sliced
1 bouquet garni
12 black peppercorns

Place the fish bones, celery, onion, carrot, leek and 2 litres (70 fl oz/8 cups) of water in a large, heavy-based saucepan. Bring slowly to the boil. Skim the surface as required and add the bouquet garni and peppercorns. Reduce the heat to low and simmer very gently for 20 minutes. Skim off any froth regularly.

Ladle the stock in batches into a sieve lined with damp muslin sitting over a bowl. To keep a clear fish stock, do not press the solids, but simply allow the stock to strain undisturbed. Allow to cool, then store in the refrigerator for up to 2 days, or in the freezer for up to 6 months. Makes about 1.75 litres (61 fl oz/7 cups).

FRENCH DRESSING (VINAIGRETTE)

3 tbsp olive oil
2 tbsp white wine vinegar
1 tsp wholegrain mustard
freshly ground pepper, to taste

Place all the ingredients in a small screw-top jar and shake well. Use immediately. Makes about 125 ml (4 fl oz/½ cup).

ITALIAN DRESSING

3 tbsp white wine vinegar
3 tbsp olive oil
½ tsp sugar
1 tbsp chopped fresh basil

Put the vinegar, olive oil and sugar in a bowl and whisk to combine. Stir in the basil and leave to stand for 15 minutes before serving. Makes about 125 ml (4 fl oz/½ cup).

MAYONNAISE

2 egg yolks
¼ tsp salt
250 ml (9 fl oz/1 cup) canola oil
½ tsp lemon juice

Put the egg yolks and salt in a bowl and whisk together until well combined and thick.

Gradually whisk in the oil, drop by drop, from a teaspoon until a quarter of the oil has been added. The mixture should be thick at this stage. Very slowly pour in the remaining oil in a thick steady stream, while continuing to beat steadily. Beat in the lemon juice. Store in a glass jar in the refrigerator for up to 3 days. Makes about 250 ml (9 fl oz/1 cup).

HINT:
• Mayonnaise can be made in a blender or food processor. Use the same ingredients as above. Blend the eggs and salt for a few seconds. With the motor running, pour in the oil in a steady thin stream. When all the oil has been added, the mixture should be thick.

MANGO CHUTNEY

1 tbsp oil
2 garlic cloves, crushed
1 tsp grated ginger
2 cinnamon sticks
4 cloves
½ tsp chilli powder
1 kg (2 lb 4 oz) fresh or frozen ripe mango flesh, roughly chopped
375 ml (13 fl oz/1½ cups) white vinegar
250 g (9 oz/heaped 1 cup) caster (superfine) sugar

Heat the oil in a heavy-based saucepan over medium heat, add the garlic and ginger and fry for 1 minute. Add the remaining ingredients and bring to the boil.

Reduce the heat to low and cook for 1 hour, or until the mango is thick and pulpy, like jam. It should fall in sheets off the spoon when it is ready. Add salt, to taste, and more chilli if you wish. Remove the whole spices.

Pour the chutney into hot sterilized jars (wash the jars in boiling water and dry them thoroughly in a warm oven). Seal the jars and allow to cool completely. Store in a cool place or in the refrigerator after opening. Makes about 500 ml (17 fl oz/2 cups).

BASIC TOMATO SAUCE

1.5 kg (3 lb 5 oz) tomatoes
1 tbsp olive oil
1 onion, finely chopped
2 garlic cloves, crushed
2 tbsp tomato paste (concentrated purée) GF
1 tsp dried oregano
1 tsp dried basil
1 tsp sugar

Score a cross on the base of each tomato, place in a bowl of boiling water for 10 seconds, then plunge into cold water and peel away the skin from the cross. Finely chop the flesh.

Heat the oil in a saucepan. Add the onion and cook, stirring, over medium heat for 3 minutes, or until soft. Add the garlic and cook for 1 minute. Add the tomato, tomato paste, oregano, basil and sugar. Bring to the boil, then reduce the heat and simmer for 20 minutes, or until the sauce has thickened slightly. Store in an airtight container in the refrigerator for up to 2 days or in the freezer for up to 6 months. Makes about 1.5 litres (52 fl oz/6 cups).

STRAWBERRY JAM

1.25 kg (2 lb 12 oz/5²/₃ cups) sugar
1.5 kg (3 lb 5 oz) strawberries
125 ml (4 fl oz/¹/₂ cup) lemon juice

Warm the sugar by spreading in a large baking dish and heating in an oven preheated to 120°C (235°F/Gas ¹/₂) for 10 minutes, stirring occasionally. Put two plates in the freezer. Hull the strawberries and put in a large pan with the lemon juice, sugar and 125 ml (4 fl oz/ ¹/₂ cup) water. Warm gently, without boiling, stirring carefully with a wooden spoon. Try not to break up the fruit too much.

Increase the heat and without boiling, continue stirring for 10 minutes, until the sugar has thoroughly dissolved. Increase the heat and boil, without stirring, for 20 minutes. Start testing for the setting point: place a little jam on one of the cold plates, a skin will form on the surface and the jam will wrinkle when pushed with a finger. It could take up to 40 minutes to reach setting point. Remove from the heat and leave for 5 minutes before removing any scum that forms on the surface. Pour into hot sterilized jars, seal and label. Makes about 1 litre (35 fl oz/4 cups).

SHORTCRUST PASTRY

190 g (6¾ oz/1¼ cups) gluten-free plain (all-purpose) flour
90 g (3¼ oz) cold butter, chopped
1 egg, lightly beaten

FOOD PROCESSOR METHOD. Put the flour and butter in a food processor and pulse until crumb-like. Add the egg and 1–2 teaspoons water until the dough is starting to come together. Don't add any more water than necessary. Turn out onto a surface lightly dusted with gluten-free flour and knead briefly to bring together the dough into a smooth ball. Wrap in plastic wrap and refrigerate to firm. Knead the dough well to help the dough hold together. Roll out between two sheets of baking paper that have been lightly dusted with gluten-free flour until large enough to line the prepared tin or dish. Refrigerate the lined dish for 30 minutes to prevent shrinkage and cracking.

BOWL METHOD. Sift the flour and icing (confectioners') sugar into a large bowl. Rub the butter into the flour with your fingertips until the mixture resembles dry breadcrumbs. Make a well in the centre and add the egg and 1–2 teaspoons water until the dough is starting to come together. Don't add any more water than necessary. Turn out onto a a surface lightly dusted with gluten-free flour and knead briefly to bring together the dough into a smooth ball. Wrap in plastic wrap and refrigerate to firm. Roll out between two sheets of baking paper that have been lightly dusted with gluten-free flour until large enough to line the prepared tin or dish. Refrigerate the lined dish for 30 minutes to prevent shrinkage and cracking.

HINTS:
• This pastry is very thin and is more difficult to handle than pastry that contains gluten. It is soft and malleable so when lining the tin or dish, fill any tears and cracks, if necessary.
• You can use margarine to make the pastry if you prefer. It will need a little less water, if any. The pastry is softer and harder to handle, but firms enough when refrigerated.
• A combination of gluten-free flours usually produces a better pastry than using only one type of flour. This is why many commercial gluten-free flour mixes contain a number of different flours.
• Sometimes gluten-free baked goods don't work because the oven is not working properly. You can check whether your oven is working properly by using an oven thermometer, which can be purchased from a good kitchenware shop.

SWEET SHORTCRUST PASTRY

190 g (6¾ oz/1¼ cups) gluten-free plain (all-purpose) flour
3 tbsp pure icing confectioners' sugar GF
90 g (3¼ oz) cold butter, chopped
1 egg, lightly beaten

FOOD PROCESSOR METHOD. Put the flour and icing sugar in a food processor and briefly pulse to combine. Add the butter and pulse until crumb-like. Add the egg and 1–2 teaspoons water until the dough is starting to come together. Don't add any more water than necessary. Turn out onto a surface lightly dusted with gluten-free flour and knead briefly to bring together the dough into a smooth ball. Wrap in plastic wrap and refrigerate to firm. Knead the dough well to help the dough hold together. Roll out between two sheets of baking paper that have been lightly dusted with gluten-free flour until large enough to line the prepared tin or dish. Refrigerate the lined dish for 30 minutes to prevent shrinkage and cracking.

BOWL METHOD. Sift the flour and icing (confectioners') sugar into a large bowl. Rub the butter into the flour with your fingertips until the mixture resembles dry breadcrumbs. Make a well in the centre and add the egg and 1–2 teaspoons water until the dough is starting to come together. Don't add any more water than necessary. Turn out onto a surface lightly dusted with gluten-free flour and knead briefly to bring together the dough into a smooth ball. Wrap in plastic wrap and refrigerate to firm. Roll out between two sheets of baking paper that have been lightly dusted with gluten-free flour until large enough to line the prepared tin or dish. Refrigerate the lined dish for 30 minutes to prevent shrinkage and cracking.

HINTS:
• The pastry is more difficult to handle than pastry that contains gluten. It is soft and malleable so when lining the tin or dish, just fill any tears and cracks, if necessary.
• You can use margarine to make the pastry. It will need a little less water, if any. The pastry is softer and harder to handle, but firms enough when refrigerated.
• A combination of gluten-free flours usually produces a better pastry than using only one type of flour. This is why many commercial gluten-free flour mixes contain a number of different flours.

Contact information for coeliac/dermatitis herpetiformis support groups

AUSTRALIA
The Coeliac Society of Australia
First Floor, 306 Victoria Avenue
Chatswood, NSW, 2067
Phone: 02 9411 4100
Email: info@coeliac.org.au
Internet: www.coeliac.org.au

CANADA
Canadian Celiac Association
5170 Dixie Road, Suite 204
Mississauga, ON L4W 1E3
Phone: 905 507 6208
Email. info@celiac.ca
Internet: www.celiac.ca

GREAT BRITAIN
Coeliac UK
Suites A-D Octagon Court
High Wycombe, Bucks HP11 2HS
Phone: 01494 437 278
Internet: www.coeliac.co.uk

NEW ZEALAND
Coeliac Society of New Zealand Inc.
PO Box 35 724
Browns Bay
Auckland 1330
Phone: 09 820 5157
Email: coeliac@xtra.co.nz
Internet: www.coeliac.co.nz

USA
Celiac Disease Foundation
13251 Ventura Boulevard, #1,
Studio City, CA 91604
Phone: 818 990 2354
Email: cdf@celiac.org
Internet: www.celiac.org